Market Smart:

How to Gain Customers and
Increase Profits with B2B Marketing

Market Smart:
How to Gain Customers and Increase Profits with B2B Marketing

Lisa Shepherd

authorHOUSE®

AuthorHouse™
1663 Liberty Drive
Bloomington, IN 47403
www.authorhouse.com
Phone: 1-800-839-8640

Published by AuthorHouse   07/13/2012

ISBN: 978-1-4772-2778-7 (sc)
ISBN: 978-1-4772-2779-4 (e)

Library of Congress Control Number: 2012911736

Contents

SECTION D: BUDGETING, MANAGING, AND MEASURING B2B MARKETING

PART TWO— IMPLEMENTING B2B MARKETING

SECTION E: DEVELOPING CONTENT

SECTION F: ONLINE TACTICS

SECTION G: OFFLINE TACTICS

CONCLUSION

IT'S TIME FOR B2B COMPANIES TO GET SMART ABOUT MARKETING

"We spent $250,000 on marketing last year, and I feel like all we got from it was a bunch of pens with our logo on them."

~Brian Stone, CEO of a $5M B2B software company

Does this sound like something you or your boss would say? If so, this book is for you.

When I meet company owners for the first time and tell them that I run a B2B strategy and marketing business, I often hear statements like the one above. Many B2B leaders have had bad experiences with marketing and many others have no experience at all. As a result, they're skeptical about marketing and feel it isn't relevant to their business, or that it's too complicated to bother with.

And that's a terrible thing. The most successful B2B companies in the world use marketing to dominate their industries and deliver enviable profits. Warren Buffett considers marketing experience pivotal in his decision to purchase a company, whether it's an insurance company (GEICO) or a railway (BNSF). Buffett says marketing strategy (he focuses on competitive advantage, a critical component of marketing strategy) is key to his investment decisions, "The key to investing is not assessing how much an industry is going to affect society, or how much it will grow, but rather determining the competitive advantage of any given company and, above all, the durability of that advantage."

In short, B2B companies need to get smart about marketing. They have the opportunity—and increasingly, the necessity—to put marketing to work for their business success. When B2B companies use marketing effectively they raise awareness of their products and services, enhance the profile of their brands, attract potential customers, and increase their profits. More and more B2B companies are getting smart about marketing—are you?

Unfortunately for many B2B companies, successful versus unsuccessful marketing is a mystery. The mystery between the two lies in the approach. Successful B2B marketers understand the importance of having a strategy, choosing and implementing the right tactics, and evolving their marketing programs as their businesses grow. Unsuccessful marketers doubt the value of a plan, dabble in marketing with a flavor-of-the-month approach, and don't tackle the challenge of measuring their results.

In my two decades of working with organizations that range from privately held B2B companies to Fortune 500 firms to not-for-profit associations, I've seen a wide variety of B2B marketing. Some of it great, much of it bad. Through that experience, I've identified the most common reasons that marketing fails in B2B companies.

Are you committing any of these seven marketing sins that lead to wasted investments and unnecessary frustration?

1. **Lacking a marketing strategy and plan.** In the excitement of launching a new product or service, it can be hard for companies to find the time to develop a plan. They have

a bias towards action—and probably deadlines to meet. Defining the target market, articulating the messaging that will attract customers, and defining the tactics that will get the company's message heard are essential efforts that are often lost in the shuffle—eventually leading to disappointing financial results.

2. **Ignoring buyer behavior.** Companies often think about products and services from their own perspective rather than from the perspective of the buyer. A product that has better technical specifications than the competitors' isn't a guaranteed success. To be truly successful, B2B marketers need to know everything about the buying process—what's important to buyers, how they buy, and who's involved in the purchasing decision. Without this knowledge, it's impossible to develop the right messages and choose the right tactics for successful marketing.

3. **Prioritizing sales and rejecting marketing.** Many B2B companies succeed in their early years by focusing on sales. At the start, it's vital to develop a track record. Direct relationships with pilot customers are the best way to develop this record. While sales is the most vital function in the early years of a B2B company, investing in sales doesn't accelerate growth the way investing in marketing does—and B2B leaders have to assess when to make the shift from adding salespeople to adding marketing resources.

4. **Failing to integrate tactics.** There is no silver bullet in marketing. One marketing tactic, used alone, is rarely as effective as when multiple tactics are used together. As the saying goes, the whole is greater than the sum of the parts. While coordinating marketing activities across tactics and channels requires effort, it brings much stronger results.

5. **Inconsistency.** Often a B2B company will launch a big marketing initiative—a website launch or a trade show

3

appearance—and then stop any marketing efforts within a few months. They'll get bored, run out of resources to manage the effort, or feel it's not worth the work because they haven't seen immediate results. Or they'll make individualized, one off marketing efforts sporadically over the year. This hot and cold approach is a terrible waste of money.

6. **Expecting instant results.** Today, business moves faster than ever—we get the status of our orders in seconds, receive month-end accounting statements in hours, and ship products in days. We want marketing to move just as fast, but relationships cannot develop in an instant and trust must be gained over time. Slow, steady progress is the key to marketing success.

7. **Not setting goals.** Marketing is a black box for many B2B leaders. They put money in, but aren't sure what comes out and don't know how to find out. Measuring marketing is not always easy, but like any business function, it must be measured. Setting goals and assessing results is the first step.

Companies waste tens to hundreds of thousands of dollars a year through these seven mistakes. If you see yourself or your organization in these sins, this book will help.

I've written this book to help B2B companies get smart about marketing. There is simply too much strong global competition for companies to sit back and wait for customers to beat a path to their door. That doesn't happen anymore—if it ever did.

What's more, the internet is changing how the business to business world works. Customers have more power and information today than ever before. This shift is increasing the importance of marketing for B2B companies. Without good marketing, B2B sales teams don't get the opportunities to present their company's solutions. While the marketing function was often ignored in B2B companies ten years ago, that's no longer the case.

My goal in writing the book is to share what I've learned over the past two decades about B2B marketing. These lessons have been developed through working with over 200 B2B organizations, both large and small. They've been learned by growing companies from under a million in revenues to multi-million dollar enterprises. My company The Mezzanine Group works with dozens of businesses every year to develop marketing strategies and manage B2B marketing programs. We know what works, and we know when, and how, to implement. Those things shift every year—as social media becomes important, learning styles change, and different buyers enter the workforce.

This book is a practical, comprehensive resource for the tens of thousands of small and mid-sized B2B companies who don't have extensive resources for marketing. While there are millions of websites and pages of resources for these companies to access on marketing, they simply don't have the time to navigate through which advice is sound and appropriate given their needs. They need a pragmatic approach to marketing, not a lot of bells and whistles. This book is heavy on pragmatism.

This book Is for two groups. It's for CEOs, owners, and leaders of B2B companies who find themselves—usually due to limited organizational resources—in charge of marketing. There are thousands of CEOs, COOs, and VPs of Business Development of B2B companies who must take charge of their company's marketing, despite having limited experience or background (and just as problematically, limited time to learn).

It's also for the thousands of coordinators, administrators and other staff who are tasked with marketing for their B2B companies, often on a part-time basis. They don't have B2B marketing training or backgrounds either, although they are often keen to learn.

How to Use this Book

There are two parts in this book. Part One is on strategy, planning, and management of B2B marketing, and Part Two covers implementation.

Part One includes:

- What business to business marketing is, how it differs from sales and consumer marketing, and why it's often hard for B2B companies to master.

- B2B marketing strategy—when and why you need to develop one and how to do so in a practical way.

- Tactical marketing planning, including a set of rules to help you evaluate which tactics are right for your business, and when.

- Guidance on managing the marketing function—how much you should spend, who should do the work, and how to measure performance.

Part Two is all about implementing B2B marketing. This section is a comprehensive, practical reference. There are tips on how to execute effectively, resources you can use, and suggested metrics for all the most commonly used B2B marketing tactics.

You can read this book cover to cover or pick and choose the sections you need. There's enough detail to provide a novice with a full understanding of B2B marketing, while an experienced marketing professional can skim for reminders on the structure and nuances of both strategy and execution.

I'd like to hear from you

Every year there are new tools and tactics. Things that were once effective stop working as well or begin working in new ways. We are constantly learning and refining. I hope the materials here, and the additional resources available at www. marketsmartb2b.com, will support you in making marketing work for your B2B company.

I'm interested in hearing your questions and experiences. As you can imagine, it's impossible to cover every situation and consideration in a single book, so I've tried to cover the most important and common issues. If you have questions that aren't covered here or an experience you'd like to share, please contact me:

Email: lisa@marketsmartb2b.com
Twitter: @MezzLisa
Blog: http://themezzaninegroup.com/blog/
The Mezzanine Group: www.themezzaninegroup.com

Good luck!

PART ONE

SECTION A:
WHAT IS BUSINESS
TO BUSINESS MARKETING?

Chapter 1— What exactly is marketing in a B2B company?

Marketing may be a major business function, but it isn't very well understood in the B2B environment. There are lots of academic definitions, but often they only make sense to those who already understand marketing. The definitions also tend to focus on B2C, rather than B2B, marketing.

I have a definition that comes from practical experience. It might not make the cut for Webster's, but for most people, it helps clarify what B2B marketing is and what it does:

> B2B marketing is *everything a company does in order to identify, generate, and support the securing of revenue opportunities.*

There are four components to B2B marketing outlined in the graphic below:

1. **Defining where and how the company will compete**: This entails the research and decisions that define the company's focus related to the markets the company participates in and its position in those markets (market intelligence and market strategy).

2. **Generating awareness and leads:** These are the activities that sit <u>at the top</u> of the sales funnel. These are often called "lead generation" or "awareness activities", as they bring in the leads that the business development team works to convert to revenues (lead generation and education).

3. **Supporting the sales process**: These are the activities that sit **alongside** the funnel and produce a positive perception of the company, as well as tangible tools and information that support the sales process (branding and sales support).

4. **Creating loyal customers**: These are the activities that sit **at the end of** the funnel and ensure that existing customers stay loyal to the company and buy again, and in greater quantities, in the future.

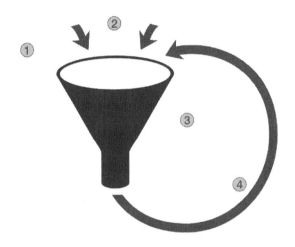

(1) **Defining where and how the company will compete:** This entails the research and decisions that define the company's focus related to the markets the company participates in and its position in those markets (market intelligence and market strategy)

(2) **Generating awareness and leads:** These are the activities that sit at the top of the sales funnel. These are often called "lead generation" or "awareness activities", as they bring in the leads that the business development team works to convert to revenues (lead generation and education).

(3) **Supporting the sales process:** These are the activities that sit alongside the funnel and produce a positive perception of the company, as well as tangible tools and information that support the sales process (branding and sales support).

(4) **Creating loyal customers:** These are the activities that sit at the end of the funnel and ensure that existing customers stay loyal to the company and buy again, and in greater quantities, in the future.

Typically, smaller companies focus on lead generation and education and branding and sales support only, while larger or more sophisticated companies focus on the market intelligence and strategy and creating loyal customers.

There is a debate surrounding the use of the funnel as an accurate depiction of the marketing development process. Those against the funnel argue that it represents a straight-line process from awareness to revenue. Such a straight-line process is no longer a reality. Today, prospects skip back and forth fluidly between stages. A prospect may be ready to buy before a salesperson has ever engaged with them.

I use the funnel here, because it's still the most widely understood conceptualization of the sales process. It may help to think of the funnel as an open structure that prospects and customers can enter and exit as they choose.

Chapter 2—What's the difference between Sales and Marketing in B2B?

There's often debate about what differentiates sales from marketing in B2B companies. Sales and marketing are incredibly intertwined and it can be difficult to draw a line between the two.

There's increasing use of the term "demand generation", which is particularly useful in early stage B2B companies. It combines sales and marketing—acknowledging the overlap between activities that are segregated at some companies.

For most companies, there does need to be a defining line between sales activities and marketing activities—particularly as the business grows and sales people become too busy to engage in marketing.

The description in the previous chapter starts the discussion about what differentiates the responsibilities of marketing and sales. Not every company follows these guideposts nor should they.

These tactics are indicated in the marketing portfolio:

ONLINE TACTICS	<ul><li>Websites</li><li>Microsites</li><li>Landing Pages</li><li>Search Engine Optimization (SEO) and Pay Per Click (PPC)</li><li>Email Marketing</li><li>Video</li><li>Webinars</li><li>Lead Nurturing Systems (Marketing Automation)</li><li>Social Media (LinkedIn, Twitter, Facebook)</li><li>Online Reputation Monitoring</li></ul>
OFFLINE TACTICS	<ul><li>Executive Seminars and Lunch and Learns</li><li>Trade Shows</li><li>Speaking Engagements</li><li>Telemarketing</li><li>Customer Appreciation Events</li><li>Direct Mail</li><li>Awards</li><li>Mass Media Tactics (TV, Radio, Out of Home)</li></ul>

These are the tactics covered in Part Two.

Ultimately, the dividing line between sales and marketing isn't important as long as the sales and marketing teams are clear on each of their responsibilities. In smaller companies, this can happen through conversations between the people involved. In larger companies, it's often spelled out in the Marketing Plan and the Business Development Plan. What's vital is that between the two groups all important activities are accounted for.

Chapter 3—How do B2B and B2C (consumer) marketing differ?

When you hear "marketing", what do you think of? Most people think of consumer marketing, the domain of Coke and Disney, Apple and Ford. Consumer marketing (Business to Consumer or B2C) is dominated by splashy, creative advertisements and massive budgets. During the Super Bowl, companies spend millions of dollars to grab the attention of viewers for just 30 seconds. That is B2C marketing.

Unfortunately, people's familiarity with B2C marketing leads to confusion and frustration with B2B marketing. While there are important consistencies between the two, there are significant differences.

B2B marketing is less about *show* (grabbing the buyer's attention in whatever way works) and more about *tell* (why is your product or service better than a competitor's?). It is vital for B2B companies to establish credibility in the eyes of target buyers. This is because B2B decisions generally carry more risk than B2C decisions. For example, if I buy a new laptop and it doesn't meet my needs, I (and I alone) bear the consequences of that decision. If I make a similar decision when buying laptops for my workplace, my colleagues and I both have to live with the consequences. And if that decision is extremely bad, not only will my colleagues be upset, but my job may be at risk or my business may suffer.

Here are some of the factors that make B2B and B2C marketing different:

B2B	B2C
• Limited number of customers and prospects • Bigger ticket purchases • Generally long buying cycles • Analytical purchase process (although not exclusively) – ROI often a driver • Multiple decision makers and influencers - purchasing, finance, engineering, operations. • Higher risk • Product or service often customized to specific buyers' needs	• Potentially millions or billions of customers • Smaller ticket purchases • Shorter buying cycles – even impulse buying • Emotional factors more likely to play a role – ROI not commonly a consideration • Often only one decision maker • Lower risk • Off the shelf product / service

Chapter 4—Why is marketing tough for B2B companies?

One of the most common questions I hear from CEOs of small and mid-size B2B companies is, "Marketing hasn't been a priority for us because of the resources required—so where do we even start?"

Their question reveals the challenges of B2B marketing. Many CEOs understand that marketing is important for their businesses, but they haven't been able to tackle it effectively. They know they should be doing it better, and they want to do it better, but they don't know how. That's understandable, because there are some significant challenges for B2B companies when it comes to marketing.

The main challenge is a resource gap. For B2B companies, marketing is rarely a core competence. In small and mid-size B2B companies, marketing is typically a small function that doesn't warrant its own executive or team. So the Head of Marketing is often someone who has another job—the CEO, the COO, or the VP of Business Development. The problem is that these executives have other priorities. If there is a problem in the plant, the COO isn't going to stop to write a press release. If there is a new sales opportunity, the VP of Sales isn't going to film a video case study. Because their other responsibilities are prioritized, marketing activities are put on hold whenever the executive is pulled away to another area, which happens frequently.

Because of the nature of marketing, this leads to poor results. Marketing is a business function that demands consistency. It's like dating—a slow and steady approach is far more effective than a courtship that blows hot and cold unpredictably. Unfortunately, many B2B companies deal with marketing in a reactive way. They ignore it until there is an issue: a trade show that's a few weeks away and hasn't been planned for, or an article that needs to be submitted to an industry journal the next morning. This leads to a huge amount of wasted marketing investment, not to mention stress, frustration, and poor representation of the company.

The other gap is one of expertise. Very few non-marketing executives have B2B marketing expertise. Heck, relatively few *marketers* have B2B marketing expertise. While there are many training grounds for B2C marketing, there are few for B2B marketing. A junior marketer within a B2B company might know about customers, buying behaviour, and industry trends, but they rarely know how to put a strategic B2B marketing plan together or how to manage the multiple moving parts it entails. There are many elements to a comprehensive marketing plan—from graphic design, to search engine optimization, to event planning, and beyond. It's challenging and rare for one person to be skilled at everything.

B2B companies are often technical in nature, and sometimes struggle to communicate the value of their products and services clearly and effectively. They are founded by someone who has technical knowledge of the service or product that the company provides. These founders are exceptionally competent in their area of expertise, and they are also pretty good salespeople—they are successful in connecting with the target market and selling their offering (or else they wouldn't still be around as a company). But marketing is not their comfort zone and they don't like the notion of promoting what they do. They often believe that if they make a product that is very, very good, customers will figure that out and come running to buy it. Sadly, that just doesn't happen.

Turnover of marketing staff is another issue for B2B companies. It is difficult to retain marketing personnel in smaller companies because of the lack of mentorship, opportunities for promotion, and the chance to constantly develop their skills. As a result, turnover of marketing personnel is high in B2B companies, which leads to gaps between marketing initiatives and too much time spent training new people.

And finally, there is confusion around tactics. It's common for one type of marketing to become the 'flavor of the month' (e.g. social media, search engine optimization, videos). Someone in a company will get excited about the potential of a tactic and will invest time or money in it. The trouble is that no single B2B marketing tactic can deliver maximum results. Making a video doesn't do anything unless the video is effectively promoted and shared with prospects. Improving search engine optimization won't help land new business if your website doesn't enable prospects to take the next step in learning more about the company. It's dangerous for B2B companies to jump on a tactic without integrating it into a cohesive marketing plan and considering if it's the right tactic for the company. For example, social media may be a hot topic, but if your industry is barely online, does it make sense for your company? You'd be surprised how many marketers fail to ask this question before "going social".

Despite these challenges, there is every reason for B2B companies to put marketing to work for them. Effective marketing builds awareness and a positive perception of the company, generates leads, and helps grow revenue. B2B companies that effectively use marketing work less to get leads and secure new business. They travel less and maintain full pricing more often. Marketing enables them to make the leap from a relatively successful company to a tremendously successful one.

So let's take the first step and talk about B2B marketing strategy.

SECTION B:
IT ALL STARTS WITH A
MARKETING STRATEGY

Chapter 5—Do you really need a marketing strategy?

Leaders of small and mid-size companies are usually action-oriented. They want to get going, to make things happen, and they don't want to wait to do it. Strategy has a negative connotation for some—it sounds like too much navel gazing and not enough getting things done. Unfortunately, when it comes to marketing, avoiding strategy is dangerous. I've seen many, many companies that just want to "get some marketing out into the market".

The problem is that they get exactly what they wish for—they get something into the market. That "something" often has no focus, no message that speaks to a desired target audience, and no follow up. It may be out there, but it doesn't do anything positive for the company. Hundreds of millions of dollars and countless hours are wasted every year in B2B marketing because of this preference towards action without planning.

On the other hand, when marketing is used strategically, a plan is set in place and executed well, it helps B2B companies clarify their competitive advantage, differentiate themselves—and most importantly—grow.

Good B2B marketing involves a roadmap. This is especially important for small and mid-size companies that have limited resources. Defining a strategy helps a company clarify its focus. What market or markets are you going after, which markets and marketing opportunities will you say no to? There are thousands of ways to spend marketing dollars. The challenge is to figure out which ways will be most effective. Most companies don't have any mechanisms for turning down marketing opportunities, so they make decisions about marketing that are ad-hoc and based on the sentiment of the decision maker in a particular moment. Companies need a strategy to focus their efforts and hold their marketing accountable for defined results.

A marketing strategy will save a company tens or hundreds of thousands of dollars by avoiding marketing activities that do not deliver the results they seek and by focusing resources in the highest value areas.

Chapter 6—What's included in a B2B marketing strategy?

To avoid that navel-gazing perception of marketing strategy, I focus on a few core elements. They address the most important aspects of B2B marketing and can be put together in a matter of days or weeks, not months. That's the practical way to form a B2B marketing strategy.

Business schools usually teach marketing strategy as "the four Ps"—product, price, place, and promotion. In my experience, the four Ps isn't a very practical definition. The reality is that most companies are fixed in their product and place (what they make and how they sell it). They can't switch from making airplane components to making farm equipment. Yes, they can introduce new products and services, but they won't make major switches. Likewise, a shift from selling through distributors to having a direct sales force is unlikely—it can happen, but it doesn't happen often.

Because of that reality, I use a different approach to defining B2B marketing strategy. I believe there are three areas that companies need to define:

- **Target Market**: Who are the ideal customers, what needs and priorities do they have, how do they make purchase decisions, and how do they learn?

- **Value Proposition**: Why should buyers buy from you? What unique factors does your company have that are important to customers? The more specific, objective, and quantified you can be, the better. This is also known as "competitive advantage".

27

- **Messaging**: This is tied to value proposition. What specific messages will you use to attract the attention of prospective buyers to convey that you understand their needs and have a solution for them?

To get answers to these questions, I use a basic framework called "the three Cs". The Cs stand for Company, Customers, and Competition. Good marketing strategy lies at the intersection of these three Cs. The next few chapters walk you through how to gather information on each of the areas and turn your knowledge into a strategy.

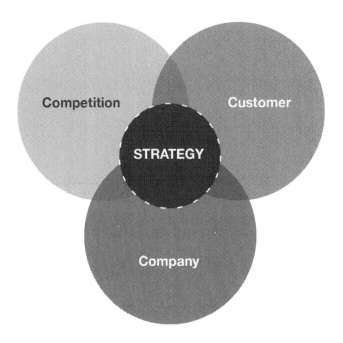

Chapter 7—How to develop a B2B marketing strategy in 3 steps

The three C's allow you to put together an effective marketing strategy quickly and clearly. It leverages the expertise that is resident in your organization and includes external research to validate and augment what is already known. There are three steps in the process:

- Step 1 is an <u>internal</u> process to gather information available within the company. It includes a company workshop and interviews with staff and management. It also collects available reports on sales, profitability, and marketing.

- Step 2 is <u>external</u>—it includes research and interviews with customers, industry experts, and competitors to augment internal information and validate, or disprove, the hypotheses you've made in Step One.

- Step 3 brings together the data and insight you've gained on the three C's to confirm the <u>marketing strategy</u>—target market, value proposition, and messaging.

> There are times when a company needs to undertake a comprehensive strategic review that involves thorough research to clarify industry trends, customer needs, and competitive offerings, as well as internal sessions to clarify strengths and opportunities. If your company is facing significant industry change or has not confirmed its business strategy for a number of years, you will first need to complete this process. Setting a marketing strategy before setting a business strategy is simply putting the cart before the horse.

The next three chapters explain how to gather company, customer, and competitor facts and insights that will serve as the platform for your marketing strategy.

> Most books talk about marketing strategy as the four P's:
>
> - Product—what will we offer?
> - Price—how much will we charge?
> - Place—where will we sell it?
> - Promotion—how will we get the word out?
>
> Most companies need to move their marketing beyond the four P's. They need to understand how to get from high level strategy to the tactical level. This book focuses on the more tactical and operational (i.e. practical) elements of B2B marketing.

Chapter 8—Clarifying your company's goals and assets

The first step in developing a solid marketing strategy is to confirm information about your company. What are your goals? Where are you relative to those goals? What do you offer? How do you make money? This chapter walks you through a practical, step-by-step process for obtaining this information.

This is an important step regardless of your company size. Sometimes the leaders of small and mid-size companies believe they know all the answers, because they're involved in the day-to-day operations of the business. What's important about this process is that it forces executives to take a step back to ask and answer broader questions in a systematic way and to get those answers down on paper—where they can be shared with others and updated periodically.

There are five questions to answer in the company assessment. Most of them are straightforward and can be accomplished through a team workshop or individual meetings with the managers and staff. Some answers will come from reports that already exist within the company.

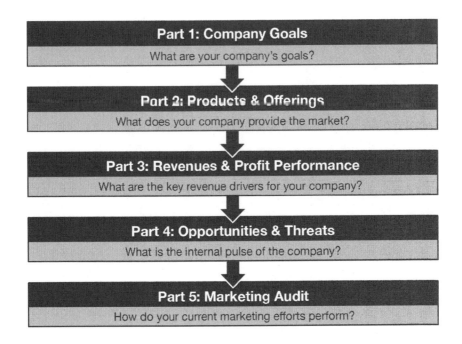

Part 1: Company Goals

What are your company's goals?

Part 2: Products & Offerings

What does your company provide the market?

Part 3: Revenues & Profit Performance

What are the key revenue drivers for your company?

Part 4: Opportunities & Threats

What is the internal pulse of the company?

Part 5: Marketing Audit

How do your current marketing efforts perform?

Part One: Company Goals

What are your company's goals? The direction you want your company to go has a big impact on what type of marketing you should engage in. Below is a list of possible business goals. Which ones apply to your company? Keep in mind these are overall business goals, not marketing goals (we'll get to the marketing goals later).

If your goals aren't on this list, don't worry—just add them.

- To become the dominant player in the market
- To position the company for strategic acquisition
- To become highly profitable with stable revenues
- To maintain market leadership
- To expand into new geographies
- To expand into new industries
- To establish channel partnerships
- To acquire a certain number of new customers

- To grow revenues among the existing client base
- To build business development and marketing capabilities
- To reach profitability

It's dangerous to select more than three or four of these goals. Prioritizing will help you focus and identify where limited resources can be invested. It can also help reveal what types and amount of marketing make sense given what you want to achieve with the business.

Part Two: Products and Offerings

Clearly defining the features and benefits that you deliver to customers is essential in developing powerful marketing. Hopefully you have a strong sense of what you provide to the market, but this process crystallizes what is different and special about each of your offerings. It will help you identify the most powerful value you provide, to whom you provide it, and the potential messages that will resonate with them.

You can do this by using a simple matrix. List your products and services across the top and then customers, technical features, and benefits down the side.

	PRODUCT X	PRODUCT Y	SERVICE X
Customer Type 1			
Features			
Benefits			
Customer Type 2			
Features			
Benefits			

Work with your team to identify all the features and benefits you provide to the different types of customers you can and do serve. Be specific, objective, and quantified. For example, stating that you provide great customer service doesn't say anything meaningful to prospects, because everyone says that Instead, specify what it is about your customer service that makes it so great. Do you guarantee that you'll have a technician available within a business day? Do you return all calls within an hour? Does your product allow customers to reduce their energy consumption by 20%? The more specific, objective, and quantified you can be, the more powerful your marketing.

Part Three: Revenues and Profit Performance

This process helps identify areas of success. It's a straight-forward exercise that pinpoints where you make your profits. It will help clarify where you want to dedicate marketing efforts and where you may not want to dedicate any effort at all.

Consider these questions:

- What is your total revenue / profit for the past 3 years?
- What is your revenue / profit by product?
- What is your revenue / profit by customer type?

The answers will reveal where your company is most successful. Every company makes investments that are expected to turn into profits in the long term. Is your company making profits where it expects to? If not, you may want to reconsider where you allocate resources, including marketing resources.

Part Four: Opportunities and Threats

Conduct internal interviews with your staff to obtain insights into perceived opportunities and threats. I'm always impressed by the depth and breadth of insight that can come from sales people, technicians, and customer service reps. Anyone who deals directly with customers has a very powerful perspective on how customers think and what they really want from your company. They often have ideas for new products or services and thoughts about emerging threats. Sitting down with these team members and having a structured conversation will allow you to capture these perspectives.

For a list of questions you can ask your team, go to www.marketsmartb2b.com/resources.

Part Five: Marketing Audit

The last step in the company assessment is to audit your marketing activities and assets. What marketing tactics do you undertake and how do they perform? How many leads does each activity generate? What tools do you have in your marketing toolkit? What collateral (brochures, tech spec sheets, project portfolios, case studies, white papers, etc) do you have? How do they represent your brand? Do they communicate your value proposition? Are they consistent?

Make sure to include these areas in your assessment:

- Website and analytics—Google Analytics, and consider using a tool like Hubspot or gShiftLabs for benchmarking data

- eNewsletters—your email provider (e.g. Constant Contact, Mail Chimp) will provide you with benchmarking data on open rates and click throughs

- Printed material—company overviews, solution overviews, and any other printed materials

- Thought leadership—articles, case studies, white papers, ebooks, videos

- Events—trade shows, webinars, and lunch and learns

- CRM system—review existing system (or lack thereof)

Compile your findings

By gathering answers to these five questions, you can establish a strong foundation. Where is the company now, what are its strengths, its assets, its opportunities? Where has it performed well in the past? Where might its opportunities lie in the future? How is the marketing function performing?

Once you've completed the assessment, take one sheet of paper and summarize your findings. This sounds easy but is often quite difficult. It can take a few rounds of work. Start by writing your key findings from each question on a page. Then work to distill the five pages down to one page of key findings. Walk away from your review for a few days and come back to it—did you miss anything important, have you included anything that isn't really essential?

Once you have the key findings, identify the implications of those findings. What do the facts mean for your business? How do you need to react to capitalize on opportunities and neutralize threats? Should you focus on a particular product line? Customer type? Is there anything you're doing that should be stopped?

And finally, store all the information you have gathered in one place—after all this effort, you should capture the information and make it easy for your team to access in future.

Chapter 9—Understanding what customers need and how they buy

The next component of the three C's model is customers. For the companies I've worked with, this step provided a tremendous amount of value. It's amazing that assessing customers and their needs could be a novel concept. But for many companies it is. The clients that Mezzanine serves are often thrilled that we will be interviewing their customers and prospects to systematically identify why and how they buy, what emerging needs they have, and what perceptions they have of the company and the competition.

The purpose of the customer assessment is to intimately understand buying behaviour. There are two ways to gather this knowledge—secondary and primary research. Secondary research relies on published information (such as industry reports) and capturing the customer knowledge that already exists in your company (sales, customer service, and management). Primary research involves conducting interviews and creating surveys directed at current or prospective customers.

Secondary Research

Secondary research is good if you need some high-level data, like the size and structure of particular industries you're considering to enter. It can help you make decisions about which industries to pursue or potential untapped markets or customer bases.

The challenge with secondary research is that there's either too much or too little. There are vast amounts of information on some industries and markets, and next to none on others—particularly at the level of depth you'll need in order to get a solid understanding of customers.

Because of this, I usually start the customer assessment process by searching online to see what's available—published reports can be useful as a starting point for areas you're not familiar with (e.g. a new geography or sector)—but be prepared to also do research on your own.

Also consider using your networks on social media such as Twitter, LinkedIn Groups, Google+, or Facebook to identify secondary data and reports that can be useful to you.

> *Sources to consider for secondary research: industry associations, local boards of trade, chambers of commerce, government bodies, and the general media (newspaper/ magazine articles, etc).*

> *Tip: If you're considering buying a report, ask for a sample in advance. Reports can sound great in the title/abstract but can let you down in the content—seeing four or five pages will give you a better sense of what you're buying.*

Primary Research

Primary research is at the heart of successful marketing strategy. It provides the necessary depth of insight. There are five steps to getting valuable customer insight.

Step One—What do you need to know?

Identify what information you want. Put a guideline together to structure your discussions with customers, prospects, and others. It will ensure you collect and capture all the great information you're about to hear. Here are the basic areas to investigate:

- *Buyer Characteristics*: What industry are they in? What kind of organization? What is their role (job title)? How long have they been in that role? What are their responsibilities?

- *Decision-Making Process*: Who's involved in making the purchase decision? Who has the power to say yes or no? When was the last purchase of this kind made? How was it made and why was a certain vendor chosen?

- *Decision Criteria*: What are the buyer's priorities? What formal or informal criteria do they have for evaluating the purchase? Is there a strict structure to the criteria or a loose framework? Are there set budgets in place?

- *Timeline*: Are purchases made on a regular basis? At what point in the business cycle does demand exist? How long is the purchase process?

- *Learning and Influences*: How do they keep up with the industry? What trade publications do they read, what industry associations do they belong to, what trade shows do they go to? Do they attend lunch and learns? Webinars? Do they read white papers? E-newsletters?

Step Two—Start with what you already know

You can complete this step at the same time as the workshop for the company assessment.

There is a tremendous amount of customer knowledge within your own company. In a workshop or individual interviews ask the sales team, customer service representatives, and management what they know or suspect. Get answers to the questions you identified in Step One. Not everyone will know everything, and they may be uncertain about particular topics, but usually a good portion of what you need to know is already resident in your company.

One caveat—your team will know a lot about your existing customers but much less about non-customers. They may also know how your customers interact with your company but not how they interact with competitors or with each other. Don't assume that what you learn from your internal sources is the full story. You will still need to do research directly among customers and non-customers to develop a marketing strategy that can help you *grow* your business both within and beyond your existing customer base.

Step Three—Conduct research

There are several methods you can use to gain and validate information on customers and prospects:

- *In-person, One-on-One Interviews* are a great way to gather in-depth insights, pain points, and issues in particular industries. In person interviews are a great way to build rapport and assess context of the answers beyond the words, such as through body language. However, this requires a substantial amount of time to properly execute and, depending on your resources and the location of your customers, this may not be a realistic option.

- *Telephone Interviews* are cost effective and avoid geographical constraints. The key with telephone interviews is the quality of the interviewee. Though you can easily speak to large volumes of people, you are better to speak with fewer, expert interviewees to gain deeper, more useful insights.

- *Focus Groups* can offer powerful insights. However, logistics can make them difficult. One way to do focus groups efficiently is to convene them around an industry conference. If everyone is going to be in the same city for a major industry event, you can often get people together for a two-hour session. You may need to offer them an incentive. You may hear different things in a group than you would one-on-one, because group-think can be a problem if your focus group isn't moderated properly.

- *Surveys* can be quick and easy, especially through online survey tools. However, the response rates are often low, which limits their value. You also must be cautious that the respondents are the people that you want to hear from. Another challenge is that many companies are not experts at developing effective survey questions, so you can end up with results that actually hurt your understanding of customer needs rather than enhance it.

Consider a third-party research company for customer and prospect research. Customers will be more truthful about your performance if they're speaking to someone outside of the company and can be confident that confidentiality will be kept.

Include satisfied customers as well as former customers in your process. And don't forget prospects—those people and companies who have never bought from you. Hearing what they know, or don't know, about your company is extremely useful. Include a spectrum of potential buyers across industries and functions to get the best possible range of perspectives.

I remember a project Mezzanine did a number of years ago for an early-stage software company. They had designed a system that allowed corporate marketing executives to manage their campaigns more efficiently and have better transparency of where cost overruns were occurring. It was an amazing system. Problem was, the company was having a very hard time selling it to the corporate marketing leaders; they just weren't interested. We did some interviews to understand their perspectives, and also talked with other executives in the corporations. Through these calls we learned that the marketing VPs weren't interested because they were pretty happy with the way things worked, and they didn't want to implement a new technology that might even shed light on where things weren't working well. The CFOs that we talked to, on the other hand, were VERY interested in the technology. They loved the transparency and the ability to see where financial inefficiencies existed. The lesson—interviewing can tell you when you're trying to sell to the wrong person.

How many interviews do you need? I find that six to eight interviews per B2B segment is sufficient in developing an understanding of the group. The challenge, of course, is that you don't know the segments before you do the interviews! But in general, twelve to thirty interviews will allow you to identify the segments and understand the differences in buying behaviour between them. The larger or more diverse your set of buyers, the more interviews you'll want to do.

Step Four—Analyze the data

It's easy to conduct primary research and then think you're done. But the raw data doesn't do much for you. It's the analysis that delivers the useful insight needed for your marketing plan.

Here are some tips to help you make the most of your research:

1. Develop hypotheses (using the internal perspectives) and use the interviews or surveys to confirm or refute the hypotheses.

2. Look for connections and patterns in the information. It's ok to use your gut to spot trends or ignore outliers, but you also need to look at the data systematically to ensure you aren't creating biases.

3. Assess what people did say as well as what they didn't.

4. Summarize key data points, notable findings, and answers to your original questions. Create charts, tables, and graphs to organize and display your findings—this is important if you are sharing your research with others.

Step Five—Identify segments

The last step is to identify the different segments that exist in the market. This is important, because it's rare that a company can serve all segments. Different segments have different needs, so it makes sense that they look to different suppliers. Defining the segments by needs will help you identify which segments you will target—and which you won't.

Segments differ based on buying characteristics. For example, if Buyer A is price insensitive, relies on consulting engineers to inform her decisions, and buys for offshore rigs, they are in a different segment than Buyer B who is primarily budget driven and buying for a small, commercial office.

For an example of customer segmentation, go to www.marketsmartb2b.com/resources.

Compile your findings

As you did at the end of the company analysis process, the last step in the Customer process is to compile your results and identify your key findings.

Chapter 10—Evaluating competitors and what they're doing

The final C is understanding the competitive landscape.

Competitive intelligence is tricky. It's hard for companies to know how much they should obtain, and it's even harder to actually obtain it. In my experience, larger companies are likely to dedicate resources to competitive intelligence (CI). Smaller companies like the idea but usually don't have the resources to commit to it. They argue that what the competition does is irrelevant, because the company is pursuing a particular direction and doesn't need to respond directly to competitors. Others believe they are small enough that they need to focus on their clients alone, not the competition.

These arguments don't hold up, because the point of CI isn't to copy the competition but rather to know what the competition is doing so that you can do <u>something different</u> that aligns with market needs and your company's strengths. A company needs to know what the competition is doing to maintain a sustainable, competitive advantage.

What information about competitors should you gather?

Basic CI includes identifying who the competition is (both direct and indirect competitors) and obtaining an overview of their characteristics: product lines, distribution, pricing, reputation, market share, business development process and team, and any other parameters you identify as crucial. You may not need to gather all of this information—select the topics that are most relevant for the competition you face and the marketing decisions you need to make.

Use a matrix to give your competitive intelligence process structure. List the competitors you're assessing along the top and the parameters along the side. When gathering information, do not use arbitrary ratings, get actual data and include it. It's important to complete the matrix in its entirety—consistency in your understanding of the competition is important so you can confidently use the information to build your strategy.

	COMPETITOR A	COMPETITOR B	COMPETITOR C
Product Lines			
Product Characteristics			
Pricing			
Other Parameters			

Gathering Information the right way

CI can sound like a sexy undertaking but don't turn it into a dumpster diving affair. There are reasonable and unreasonable ways to do CI. The latter can land companies in the headlines and are more likely to hurt than help.

In most cases, a third party is needed to obtain competitive intelligence. They can get access to details and people that you cannot simply by merit of being independent. This method requires the most financial commitment, but often it is the only viable solution for getting useful CI.

The simplest starting point for CI (although it's just the starting point, not the be-all and end-all) is online. Looking at a competitor's website can provide a baseline of information, including marketing collateral (brochures, press releases, etc.). These can be revealing—are competitors expanding into a new region? Opening a new distribution centre? Launching a new product?

However, be wary of what you find online. Many companies, especially smaller and mid-size, don't keep their sites up to date, and how they look online may be entirely different from reality.

Check for posted job opportunities. Learning about the type of people your competition is hiring can give you clues to what market niches they are exploring, which divisions they are expanding, and what product or service lines they are prioritizing. Social media such as LinkedIn can be a great resource to understand who's moving into (or out of) a competitor.

Ask your business development team. Their direct contact with customers provides them access to strong market knowledge. Leverage their relationships with customers to assess the competition. Ask for their objective opinions.

Look for former employees on LinkedIn. As long as they are not under confidentiality agreements, they may be able to share some insight.

Consider talking with head-hunters, industry association personnel, or other industry watchers who may have views on the industry. You'll be amazed by what people will tell you, if only you ask.

Mystery shopping will sometimes work for B2B companies. Buy something from your key competitors to understand every facet of their customer experience. Are they responsive? What is their sales process? Do they provide follow up after the sale? Although this method allows you to gather data via personal, first-hand experience, it is quite tricky, because it isn't always possible to buy something from your competition and when you can, it will involve an investment.

Most importantly—ask customers. They almost always have useful knowledge of your competition and are often willing to share.

Finally, don't make the mistake of using your competitive intelligence in a reactive way. If your company's competitive advantage lies in a unique product or service quality, don't alter your core strategy just because your competitor is altering theirs. Focus on your own strengths and customer needs.

Once you have completed the competitive intelligence, do the same analysis as the one you did at the culmination of the company and customer steps. What are the key findings, what are the strengths and weaknesses of competitors, what direction are they heading in, and what might it mean for your company?

Chapter 11—Defining your marketing strategy

Now that you have gathered a full view of your company, customers, and competition, you can develop the marketing strategy.

Start by summarizing the results of the three C's. In each section, you created a few pages of key findings and implications. Put all of these together and evaluate them as a whole. What do can you take away from them? Did you learn from the company analysis that your organization has the largest market share, and one segment of your customers values buying from a stable supplier? If so, perhaps one of your main marketing messages should be that your company is the largest supplier of your product or service and, as a result, you provide stability and economies of scale. If you identified through your analysis that no company has established a leadership position in a particular market, there may be an opportunity for your company to become leader.

One tool that is helpful in clarifying your marketing strategy is a SWOT framework. Here are a few questions to consider in assessing your strengths, weaknesses, opportunities, and threats:

Capitalize on STRENGTHS	Diminish WEAKNESSES
• Where are you successful? Why? How can this area grow? • Are there elements of your offering that clients particularly value that you could better promote? • Have you created a new process or product that perfectly meets customer needs?	• Where are you losing share or money? Why? • Are your competitors taking share – which segment are they focusing on and with what value proposition? • Can this area be improved or should it be eliminated? • Are there knowledge and/or capability gaps?
Pursue OPPORTUNITIES	**Mitigate THREATS**
• Are customers demanding solutions that fit your company's existing capabilities or capabilities you could develop? • Where are your competitors losing? Why? Can you pick up their dissatisfied customers by promoting a particular service or benefit? • Are there emerging markets that are lucrative for you to pursue?	• Where are competitors heading? Do you have the resources to compete with them? Do you want to? • Are there changes in market demand? Any new entrants? Are there new regulations that will affect the industry?

1. **Capitalize** on Strengths
    - Where are you successful? Why? How can this area grow?
    - Are there elements of your offering that clients particularly value that you could better promote?
    - Have you created a new process or product that perfectly meets customer needs?

2. **Diminish** Weaknesses
    - Where are you losing share or money? Why?
    - Are your competitors taking share—which segment are they focusing on and with what value proposition?
    - Can this area be improved or should it be eliminated?
    - Are there knowledge and/or capability gaps?

3. **Pursue** Opportunities
   - Are customers demanding solutions that fit your company's existing capabilities or capabilities you could develop?
   - Where are your competitors losing? Why? Can you pick up their dissatisfied customers by promoting a particular service or benefit?
   - Are there emerging markets that are lucrative for you to pursue?

4. **Mitigate** Threats
   - Where are competitors heading? Do you have the resources to compete with them? Do you want to?
   - Are there changes in market demand? Any new entrants? Are there new regulations that will affect the industry?

Now you're ready to define the marketing strategy. As I mentioned previously, I don't think the four Ps are relevant to most companies at this stage. What's more relevant are these three areas:

1. **Target Market(s):** Who are the target markets (usually segments within the overall market) that you're going to pursue? Which segment(s) best fit your company's capabilities, strengths, and goals? Which segment will you pursue first, and then next? You can't pursue them all; this activity is all about prioritizing.

2. **Value Proposition**: Why should people buy from you instead of your competitors? What are your specific, objective, and quantified competitive advantages for each of your target markets (they usually differ between segments). Be very clear here—don't fall back on business jargon or vague statements.

3. **Messaging:** What words will you use to spark interest among your target market? Your messaging will be based on your value proposition. The focus should be on pain

points—your messaging needs to address your target market's pains.

These exercises are the practical approach to developing an effective marketing strategy. You should be able to present your strategy in ten to fifteen PowerPoint slides—or six to nine pages of text. If it's longer, you need to continue refining it.

> *The hardest part of defining strategy for small and mid-size B2B companies is saying "no" to some types of customers and some potential opportunities. It's difficult, but this is where the value lies. For B2B companies with limited marketing resources, it's essential to dedicate sufficient effort in the areas with the best potential. This doesn't mean you won't accept business from customers who aren't in your target markets; it simply means you aren't investing resources to pursue them.*

Want an example of a marketing strategy to guide you? Download one from www.marketsmartb2b.com/resources.

Your strategy is the foundation for all your marketing activities. However, it's only the foundation. The next section will teach you how to turn this foundation into effective marketing actions.

SECTION C:
MOVING FROM STRATEGY
TO REALITY: TACTICAL PLANNING

Chapter 12—What is a tactical B2B marketing plan?

Without a strategy, marketing tactics are often just a haphazard collection of ideas. But B2B marketing effectiveness lies in translating that strategy into action through tactical planning.

A tactical B2B marketing plan outlines:

- ***What* will be executed**—A clear list of the marketing tactics that will be undertaken based on the marketing goals.

- ***When* tactics will happen**—A calendar that outlines the timing of tactics and activities.

- ***Who* will be responsible for implementing**—A detailed schedule of the amount of time and other resources required along with responsibilities for who has input and who is in charge.

- ***How much* money will be spent**—The budget for each tactic.

- ***Why* the tactic is being undertaken**—How performance will be measured, primarily the outcomes and metrics the team will use to gauge success.

Developing the tactical plan helps prioritize the marketing tools and initiatives that will fulfill your objectives.

A solid tactical plan is essential for managing the marketing function—without one, it's difficult to monitor performance and determine whether you're making progress.

In this section, I describe how to create the components of the tactical plan—how to choose tactics, create a realistic timeline, and determine the resources required. In the last section, we'll cover budget and performance measurement.

Chapter 13—How do you choose the right tactics for your company?

One of the most common challenges for B2B companies is knowing which marketing tactics they should implement. They might hear about a particular tactic, jump on the bandwagon, and then when it doesn't work out, they proclaim, "Marketing doesn't work for our company". Or they might stick with a tactic, because it's common in their industry, or it's the way things have always been done. These techniques lead to ineffective marketing, because a good strategy is all about choosing the right tactics at the right time.

Almost every B2B company wants a standard prescription for marketing tactics. I wish there was such an easy answer. But many factors influence which marketing tactics a company should use:

-   The industry
-   The target market
-   The company's position in the market
-   How much marketing the company has done in the past and how successful it has been
-   What kind of marketing the competition does
-   The company's goals
-   The company's marketing budget

I have four guidelines to help companies choose the right tactics.

Guideline 1: Get the basics in place

In my experience, B2B companies focus mainly on sales and product development when starting out. Marketing isn't a major consideration, but some marketing basics are needed to legitimize the company and support the sales team in securing early stage customers. The marketing basics vary by industry but usually include a website (that accurately reflects the company's solutions and value), a company overview, and product technical specification sheets. Other tools that can be helpful include product demonstration videos, ROI calculators, case studies, and testimonials.

For any B2B company, no matter how small, these are the essentials.

Guideline 2: What's your stage of evolution?

Different B2B marketing tactics have impact at different stages of growth—some deliver incredible ROI at one stage and none (or negative) at another. I use this rough framework to guide what marketing investments a B2B company should consider:

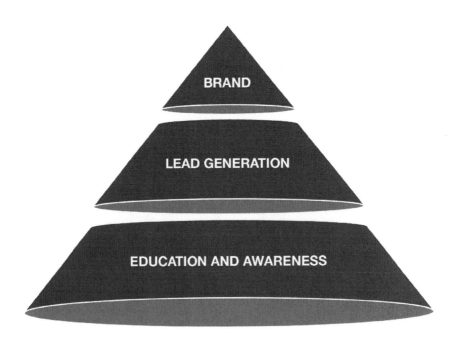

The main areas are education and awareness, lead generation, and brand building. This framework is a rough outline—there aren't always clearly defined lines between stages.

Phase 1—Education and Awareness

The early stages of most B2B marketing are typically focused on getting pilot clients. The target market doesn't know the company—and in many cases doesn't even know that their solution exists—so it's the role of sales and marketing to educate the market and raise awareness. In Phase 1, marketing investments should educate the market and generate awareness, such as video demonstrations, white papers, telemarketing, and speaking engagements. In some industries, social media works well at this stage. Unless a B2B company is venture-funded and has very aggressive growth goals, the marketing investments should be narrowly focused at this stage. Marketing's primary role is to support the company in securing enough pilot clients to create a track record.

Phase 2—Lead Generation

Once a B2B company has a track record and a story to tell, it can move into a more aggressive expansion period where marketing is looked to for higher ROI. There is no hard line indicating when a company has arrived at this stage, generally an organization will have a sense of confidence that they have enough proof of concept and reference clients to assert themselves in the market. At this stage, B2B companies should add marketing activities that focus on generating leads and leveraging the awareness that was built during Phase One. Examples include SEO, lead nurturing systems, and webinars. To support these activities, more time must be spent on content development to provide the inputs for the marketing activities.

Phase 3—Brand Building

Just like with one and two, there is no hard and fast line between Phase 2 and Phase 3. A B2B company in Phase 3 has reached a point where it seeks to dominate its industry. Marketing becomes a major investment in order for the company to solidify its brand position. The tactics that it will undertake may be more complex and long-term oriented, such as sponsorships. There is powerful value in being a Phase 3 B2B company—these organizations move to value selling and garner premiums for their expertise and brand rather than purely the widget they produce. The expectation should be that the company gets sole-sourced and is able to secure price premiums over the competition.

On the following page is a chart that suggests the main B2B marketing tactics and the marketing goals they fulfill. Keep in mind, every industry varies, so this is only a guideline.

	MARKETING BASICS	EDUCATION & AWARENESS	LEAD GENERATION	BRAND BUILDING
Websites	✓✓	✓✓	✓✓	✓✓
Microsites			✓	✓
Landing Pages		✓	✓✓	✓
SEO	✓	✓	✓✓	✓
PPC		✓	✓✓	✓
Email Marketing	✓	✓	✓✓	✓
Webinars		✓	✓✓	✓✓
Social Media		✓	✓	✓✓
Executive Seminars		✓	✓✓	✓✓
Trade shows		✓	✓✓	✓✓
Speaking Engagements		✓	✓✓	✓✓
Telemarketing	✓	✓	✓	
Customer Appreciation Events				✓✓
Direct Mail		✓	✓	
TV, Radio, OOH			✓	✓✓
Sales Support Collateral	✓✓	✓		
Public Relations	✓	✓✓	✓✓	✓✓
Awards		✓	✓	✓✓

Guideline 3—Prioritize Tactics by ROI

Marketing tactics should be chosen based on the results they can deliver, starting with the highest potential ROI to the lowest. The highest value revenues usually come from selling existing products or services to existing customers and the lowest from selling new products or services to new customers—as in the chart below:

MARKETING TACTIC ROI		Product / Services	
		Existing	New
Customers	New	$$	$
	Existing	$$$$	$$$

So what can you do to promote existing products to existing customers? Email is a good choice for staying in touch with customers, keeping them abreast of technical improvements, telling them about new applications for your solutions, and generally reminding them that you exist.

After that, the highest value comes from selling new products to existing customers. Your existing base should be the target for product launches. Invite them to upcoming lunch and learns or webinars to showcase your latest innovations.

Then you can focus on promoting existing products to new customers. Here is where you'll consider tactics like SEO.

And finally, pursue new revenues among new customers. This can be done through, for example, trade shows.

What's interesting is that most companies put this last category first when they think about marketing. But this isn't the place to start, when maximizing ROI is your goal.

Admittedly, this framework isn't entirely black and white. Many tactics cross between quadrants. A trade show might touch all four tactics. All the same, it's a good guideline for evaluating the right tactics for your B2B company.

Guideline 4: Focus Your Efforts and Evolve

The final consideration when choosing tactics is this: don't try to do too much at once. If you try to do too much, you'll end up doing a poor job of everything. You're better off beginning with a handful of tactics that are clearly aligned with your goals, and focusing your effort on executing those tactics well. If you're just starting out in marketing, pick three to five tactics over your first six months. More sophisticated companies, or those who are leveraging outside support and expertise, can work with five to twelve. If you do a good job implementing your priority tactics, you'll get results—and that will enable you to evolve your marketing program with confidence—and higher profits.

Chapter 14—Integrating tactics to nurture B2B relationships

There is no silver bullet in B2B marketing. While individual tactics are effective methods of increasing exposure and driving leads, no tactic alone is as effective as multiple tactics used together. All B2B marketing tactics are more effective when used as part of an integrated marketing plan. B2C companies create television, radio, digital, and print marketing efforts to make sure consumers hear their message frequently and repeatedly; similarly, B2B companies need to integrate their tactics to build awareness of their solutions.

For example, a telemarketing campaign might work for your business, but it will be much more effective if combined with an email that informs the recipient that you'll be calling, an invitation to an upcoming webinar, and then a follow-up invitation to an event at a local, industry trade show. The golden rule is that it takes five to seven touches before your name will register on the typical, busy person's radar. So integrating tactics is essential to get B2B buyers to hear and understand your message.

The other reason to integrate tactics is that it enables your company to nurture relationships. The B2B purchase cycle is long, so it's unlikely to land on a potential buyer's radar and have them buy the next week. B2B relationships must be nurtured over time, providing the right type and amount of information and expertise to move prospects one step further in the sales process. Integrating tactics enables you to do this—you can provide a white paper, a webinar, an email newsletter with recent case studies, and an invitation to a local lunch and learn over the course of weeks or months. This allows you to build relationships with prospects. The growing number of lead-nurturing systems makes it much more cost effective than in the past—see Chapter 37 for more on lead nurturing.

Lead nurturing is getting more interesting these days, as the traditional "funnel" model (or AIDA—awareness, interest, desire, action) is breaking down. While the process is less predictable from stage to stage, there are still steps. Good marketing must cover all the steps and make the information available for prospects at every stage of the purchase process, regardless of the order they happen in.

Chapter 15—How do you create a realistic action plan?

Putting together a marketing calendar requires realistic thinking about what tactics you can undertake with your resources. If you're using an outside firm or firms to support your marketing, you have an advantage in that they will carry the bulk of the workload. But don't assume that your time won't be needed—it will. No outside firm can undertake B2B marketing in a vacuum. If they try, they won't be able to create as valuable of a product—they simply won't have enough of your technical knowledge to develop and distribute the content that is needed to establish you as a leader.

I suggest two ways for developing a realistic marketing calendar. The first is the "work-back" plan:

a) Determine your **total capacity**. For example, if you have a part-time marketing resource (half of an FTE), your marketing capacity is roughly eighty hours per month.

b) Identify your **fixed marketing activities**—the major industry conferences, trade shows, and other events. Enter these on your marketing calendar along with relevant deadlines, such as the deadline for shipping the booth.

c) Identify the **tactics** related to those fixed events and estimate the time needed for them.

   • If you're using your own resources for marketing, especially if you're starting marketing with minimal infrastructure in place, be prepared for tasks to take longer than predicted. To be safe, add 10-20% to the amount of time you've initially estimated.

- Think about the inputs to the fixed events—for example, are you rebranding and need to incorporate the new corporate identity into the trade show materials? These need precede the other activities, so make sure to add them to your critical path.

d) Earmark 10% of your total capacity to **allow for marketing opportunities** that arise—they always do. Leave more if your company is growing rapidly.

e) Calculate your **remaining capacity** by subtracting the time required for fixed activities (step c) and for unallocated activities (step d) from your total capacity (step a).

f) Identify your **remaining marketing tactics** and the amount of time needed to execute them. Enter them on the calendar until you've run out of capacity.

This approach helps companies be realistic about marketing resources and what can be accomplished. The drawback is that it's possible to allocate time and resources to the wrong tactics—for example, what if the fixed events shouldn't, in fact, be the highest priority tactics?

The second approach is the "work-up" plan:

a) Identify the marketing that you want to do from **highest priority** to lowest.

b) **Estimate the amount of time** required for individual tactics.

c) **Enter tactics and hours** on the calendar, respecting the fixed events (time-specific, third-party events) and building tactics around them as appropriate.

d) **Spread out your marketing initiatives** over the year to balance out capacity as much as possible, recognizing that some activities simply have to be done at certain times.

e) Evaluate what amount of **resources you need**—is it a part-time resource, full-time resource, a number of vendors?

This approach helps identify what resources are needed to execute your marketing tactics. The drawback—very few companies have the resources to do everything they want to do.

I find a combination of these two approaches is the best way to get a realistic calendar that prioritizes the right tactics.

To download a template for a marketing calendar, go to www.marketsmartb2b.com/resources.

Most companies need three to six months of operating with their marketing calendar to have a strong sense of what they can really accomplish. The efficiency and project management skills of your marketing resources will determine how much can be accomplished.

SECTION D:
BUDGETING, MANAGING,
AND MEASURING B2B MARKETING

Chapter 16—What should your B2B marketing budget be?

So how much should you spend on marketing? There is surprisingly little standard information on this topic. It's one of the most common questions I hear from CEOs—they simply don't know what's reasonable.

Every company has a different approach to marketing and needs different tactics, therefore a different marketing budget is needed for every company. Factors that affect a company's marketing budget include the nature of its industry, its business goals (especially related to growth targets), the size and stage or evolution of the company, its target market, the position it wants to take in the industry, and its distribution model.

With those caveats, here are some guidelines. The 2012 Marketing Sherpa study of 1,745 B2B marketers provides the following benchmarks:

- 48% of B2B companies spend 1-5% of gross revenue on marketing
- 25% of companies spend 6-10% of gross revenue on marketing
- The remaining 27% of B2B companies spend more than 10%

This is a good guideline for companies that are newer to the marketing function. If you are just starting out, allocate in the 1-5% range, and as you build competence, you'll have every reason to expand. Companies that are more sophisticated, and understand how to get ROI from marketing, tend to increase their spend from year to year—which makes sense, because as they make more money through marketing, they want to do more of it.

Many companies wonder about the breakdown between marketing staff and marketing programs (e.g. trade shows, print advertising, pay-per-click, SEO). This metric used to be a good gauge of the efficiency of a marketing team. Companies would aim to get their staff costs down to a percentage of total budget. Smaller companies tended to have staff costs around 50%, and larger companies (with larger spend and therefore efficiency) would spend closer to 20%.

The 2012 Marketing Sherpa study indicated that 70% of the 1,745 B2B company participants spent between 5% and 30% of their budget on in-house staff. The remaining 30% of firms spent 30% to 90%.

This data demonstrates a shift in marketing behaviour. B2B tactics that involve labour (e.g. content development and social media) are on the rise, while tactics that involve tangible goods (e.g. brochures and pens) are in decline. I expect this shift will continue, and there will be fewer questions around the breakdown of budgets and more questions on overall ROI. At the end of the day, it's all about how much profitable revenue the marketing program generates.

Chapter 17—Who should do the marketing?

Small and mid-size B2B companies face a challenge in finding the right level and amount of resources to effectively manage marketing, as I discussed in Part One.

There are several options for B2B companies to get the right resource mix for effective marketing. The graphic below demonstrates how the extent and sophistication of marketing activities give a guideline for what kind of human resources are needed.

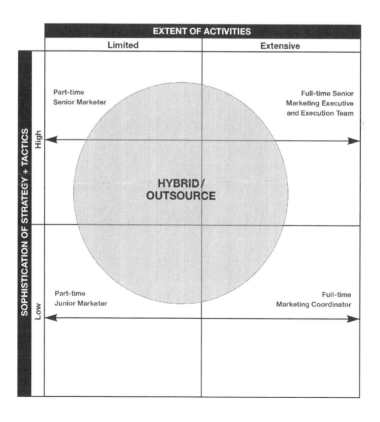

The previous chart illustrates the following approaches to resourcing marketing in a B2B company:

- In-house, full-time senior marketer (e.g. VP or CMO)
- In-house, full time junior marketer (e.g. coordinator or manager)
- Mix of part-time, in-house junior and senior marketers
- Part-time, senior independent contractor
- Hybrid solution (outsourced marketing management)

In-house Senior Marketer (VP, CMO)

Having an in-house senior marketing executive is an aspiration for many B2B companies. An executive responsible for marketing allows the company to have marketing expertise (assuming the right person was hired) to make good, strategic decisions about marketing investments. It means that someone at the leadership level is bringing marketing issues to the fore, and these issues are being considered when making investments in other departments (e.g. the marketing impact of customer service decisions).

However, the majority of small and mid-size B2B companies don't need, and can't afford, a senior marketing executive. Their salary isn't justified based on the marketing spend and needs of the company. So, while having a marketing executive is appealing for small and mid-size B2B companies, for most it's not practical. Companies that have over fifty million in revenue and spend more than one million annually in marketing usually need senior marketing leadership. Below this level, it depends on the company's strategy and industry.

In-house Junior Marketer (Coordinator, Manager)

When most B2B companies begin to get serious about marketing, they start out by hiring someone at a junior level. A full-time junior marketer can do a lot—and there is usually a lot to be done.

But the downside to junior marketing personnel is that they often don't have strategic marketing skills. They don't know which marketing tactics make sense given the company's overall business strategy. They must be managed and directed by a manager in the company, which can be challenging if that manager has a busy schedule. Junior marketing personnel are also more likely to leave the company. If they are focused on developing their careers, they will crave opportunities to take on new challenges, which they may achieve by jumping from one company to the next. This is difficult because it creates gaps between marketers, which brings inconsistency in execution. Management will need to dedicate time to identifying and then orienting new personnel.

And, of course, there's the challenge of finding good junior talent—people with a great work ethic and the ability to fit into the culture of a particular organization.

Senior / Junior Mix

Having a combination of senior and junior marketers is a good way to achieve strategic marketing that is consistently executed. The senior marketer should be responsible for setting the strategy, determining tactics, investment levels and the scorecard, and advocating for marketing within the company's leadership team. The senior person should also handle some of the execution activities, such as setting up strategic alliances and the thought leadership program. The junior marketer will be responsible primarily for execution and should be overseen by the senior.

The drawback to this approach is that many B2B companies simply don't need two full-time marketing resources given the limited size of their marketing program.

Part-Time Senior Independent Contractor

One way for a B2B company that doesn't have an extensive marketing program to achieve the level of strategy needed is to contract a senior independent marketer. If the company can find a marketing executive who has relevant experience, and retain them on an ongoing, part-time basis, they can access the expertise they need. To make this work, a coordinator or manager will also be needed to handle execution, as the senior person will not be cost effective (and likely not interested) in this component of the marketing function.

There are two potential drawbacks to this approach. The first is sustainability. If the independent contractor is between jobs and takes a full-time role with another company, you may be left without a resource and have to start the process of finding a marketer all over again. The second is a question of skill. Does the independent have experience and knowledge in the tactics that make sense for your company? If not, they are likely to adopt the tactics they have experience in—and these might end up wasting your investment rather than growing your business. Be sure to vet any independents before retaining them to ensure they have the skills and experience to direct your marketing appropriately.

Hybrid Solution (outsourced marketing management)

There are B2B marketing outsourcing firms that provide a strategic marketing plan developed by a team of experts, and then the resources to execute the plan on an ongoing basis. My company, The Mezzanine Group, provides this kind of service.

This model is fairly new and different companies have different approaches. Some work on-site at the client's location, others work off-site. Some handle everything under a full-service model, others do certain pieces but will also use clients' admin or junior staff.

This approach gives B2B companies access to marketing strategy expertise and then resources to execute cost efficiently. They can provide better marketing results, because they know what tactics to use and how to implement them. They're more accountable than in-house staff because of the nature of their contracts with clients, and they enable the company's management team to devote less time to managing marketing than would be possible with an in-house solution.

The downside is that they cost more than an in-house marketing resource on an hour-for-hour basis.

Chapter 18—Systems to make marketing efficient

Like every business function, marketing performs best when it is actively managed. Most B2B companies don't do a good job of consistently managing their marketing. They find they don't have time, and then wonder why their marketing isn't performing well. If you're taking the time to read this book, I assume you're interested in achieving effective marketing. Proper management is the place to start.

The building blocks of effective marketing management are:

a) Have a marketing plan to guide activities and clarify goals
b) Dedicate an appropriate level and quantity of resources (time, money)
c) Meet weekly to review and discuss progress with the people who are executing
d) Recalibrate the plan as needed to respond to opportunities and challenges
e) Report activities and results on a monthly basis (more on that in Chapter 19)

Easy, right? Somehow it's tougher in reality, but having the right senior resources will address the common challenges in marketing management. One of the best methods, once you have a marketing plan and someone responsible for executing it, is holding weekly meetings (building block c). Doing this will make it clear—quickly—if you have the right resources for your marketing and whether or not your plan is doable.

Be flexible in your approach if you're new to marketing. Market conditions can change, new forces can affect buyer behaviour, and other, unforeseen circumstances can affect your marketing program. Be prepared to reassess, recalibrate, and adjust timing of marketing tactics as you proceed with implementation and are regularly measuring performance. Below are a few tips and questions to ask over the course of the year to ensure that your marketing is adapting to changes in conditions

- Is your marketing achieving the goals you set (see Chapter 19)?

- Which tools and tactics are working and which aren't?

- Are some tactics delivering better results than others? If so, can you move budget and activity into those areas and away from others?

Timing
In the majority of B2B environments where the sales cycle is long and complex, it takes time for marketing to make an impact. Here are a few timing guidelines—these are general and your specific experience may be different.

1-8 WEEKS — Marketing ACTIVITY
- Press releases
- Website updates

4-12 WEEKS — Marketing RESULTS
- Media mentions of stories in industry publications
- Better search engine rankings

6-24 WEEKS — Increase in LEADS
- Visibility of marketing efforts will generate awareness and interest

8-52 WEEKS — Increase in DEALS
- Larger deals will take more time

- It will take 1-8 weeks to see marketing activity (e.g. press releases, website updates)

- It will take 4-12 weeks to see marketing results (better search engine rankings, media mentions of stories in industry publications)

- It will take 6-24 weeks to see an increase in the number of leads

- It will take 8-52 weeks to see new deals as a result of marketing (typically, the bigger the deals, the longer it takes)

If your initial results aren't hitting your targets, it doesn't necessarily mean you're on the wrong track. It does take time, and finding the right mix of marketing tactics is a balance that few companies get perfect the first time around. After two to three months, sit down and evaluate what you've been doing, how well you've been executing, and what the results are. If things are going in the right direction but aren't delivering the quantity of results you're looking for, you may need to devote more time to marketing.

If you feel you aren't executing well, take a look at your resources and plan—are you trying to do too much with too little? If you aren't getting any good results and things don't seem to be going in the right direction, look at the deeper issues—is your strategy (business or marketing) sound, are you using the right tactics, is your message on the mark? Then recalibrate your plan and keep going.

Chapter 19—How to set goals for B2B marketing

There are two things to measure in B2B marketing—activities and results. Some companies argue that all that matters is results, and indeed, that's ultimately true, but it's easier to evaluate the results when you know the level of activity being applied.

It's important to balance the measurement of both activities and results. I've seen many companies get distracted by the amount of marketing activity and forget about getting results. I've also seen companies expect significant results and then not execute the activities. Both matter.

It would be nice if there was a standard prescription for setting marketing goals. Unfortunately, there isn't. However, in the sections on tactics, I provide a number of metrics that address both the activity and result considerations.

You can compile the individual tactic metrics into a marketing scorecard that includes five to ten metrics that you will track and report on monthly. Some metrics may be leading indicators (for example, leads will help predict revenues) and others will be lagging. The purpose is to focus your marketing team on the activities that matter most to your business success and for everyone to get a view into what results are being achieved.

For an example of a marketing scorecard, go to
www.marketsmartb2b.com/resources.

PART TWO

Part Two, the majority of this book, is dedicated to implementing B2B marketing tactics. There are 3 sections.

The first covers content development (also called "thought leadership"), the fuel that drives B2B marketing. There are a number of chapters on developing different types of B2B content, everything from case studies to videos.

The next two sections cover each tactic. They're grouped into online tactics and offline tactics, although there are some (like PR) that cross between the two.

Each chapter provides an overview of the tactic, some tips on how to implement effectively, and suggested metrics. While there are a few tactics I haven't covered, I've tried to address the most prevalent and critical ones for B2B companies.

SECTION E:
DEVELOPING CONTENT

Chapter 20—Why do you need content?

One of the biggest differences between B2B and consumer marketing is thought leadership. A thought leader is a company or individual recognized for their expertise in a particular area. A thought leader can guide their industry towards the implementation and application of new ideas. Being recognized as a thought leader makes you the "go-to" for particular products or services and is a powerful way to increase brand equity, achieve price premiums, and avoid bid competition.

B2B companies need to be thought leaders in order to dominate their industries. But how do you become recognized as a thought leader?

The starting point is to have deep expertise in a particular area and a demonstrated track record. If you don't have proof that your solution works, your first step is to get that proof. Without it, buyers won't have any evidence of your expertise or qualifications—making it less likely that they'll choose to buy from you. This means that any marketing you do without a track record might be dollars badly spent.

Once you have a track record, the next step is to establish your reputation as a thought leader. This happens by sharing your experience and expertise through content, such as white papers, case studies, blogs, and articles.

Generating content is simple to plan but much harder to execute. I've seen many companies recognize the importance of generating content, commit to it whole-heartedly, and then fall on their faces within three months. I'll even admit that one of those companies was Mezzanine in its early years.

The good news: it gets easier with experience, but it takes continued commitment and resources, and some systems and processes.

There are two parts to content development—deciding what content to produce and producing it.

Chapter 21—How do you decide what topics to cover?

Some companies struggle with what kind of content to produce—they don't realize they have expertise that can be turned into compelling material. Here are some practical ways to identify and qualify content ideas:

1. Generate a list of twenty topics and **ask your customer-facing staff** (business development, customer service) to rate the topics. Since these employees talk with customers every day, they understand what's important to them. They know what questions they get asked, and they know what is currently selling.

2. Repeat the process of gathering topics, but have a **customer advisory panel** rate the topics. A customer advisory panel usually consists of five to ten customers that have a good relationship with your company and that represent your full customer base. Send each customer a personalized email and have them rate each topic. Most importantly, make it dead easy for them. The process should only take five minutes of their time; you're looking for a gut reaction to the topics.

3. Take your **product developers** (often engineers) to lunch, talk to them, and take notes. During these lunch meetings, get the engineers to talk about your products or services; their passion and enthusiasm for the product will come across naturally. If you are in a highly technical industry, get them to explain the most technical aspects of the product and why they're useful to customers. After

you've spoken to several different engineers, gather up your notes and create content ideas.

As a final step, cross-reference your topic list against upcoming product launches, your firm's core competencies, market trends, and changing customer needs to ensure the topics are well-aligned with your strategy.

Through this process, create an editorial calendar for the year. What topics will you cover and when? Should some topics come before others? Are some topics relevant at particular times of the year or business cycle?

Chapter 22—How do you produce content?

The reality of B2B marketing is that content needs to come, in good measure, from the thought leaders. Unfortunately, they don't always enjoy the process of disseminating their expertise. Ask an engineer to write a white paper, and he or she will be happy to do it—but you'll be lucky to see it within a few months.

The best way to produce content for B2B marketing is to make it very easy for the technical experts to contribute—which means not forcing them to produce content all alone.

A good approach is to choose a topic and interview a technical expert for thirty to sixty minutes, capturing as much knowledge as possible, and then prepare a first draft of the piece. It won't be perfect, but it will be something the expert can respond to. Book more time with him or her and get verbal feedback. Then do another draft and work this way, on a timeline, until completion.

Another approach is to hire a third party to develop the content. The pressure of having someone else involved can be a good motivator to keep the technical experts moving.

Chapter 23—Sales Support Collateral

Every B2B company needs basic collateral that supports the sales team when presenting to potential customers. However, the nature of those materials has changed over the last decade. The extensive, glossy brochures of the past are no longer the norm, and it's more likely that the sales team will need digital versions of their materials to send prospects before and after sales meetings.

One of the most common sales support documents is a professionally prepared overview of the company with information on its history, management team, expertise, and solution set (products, services, or combination).

Technical specification sheets are still common in engineered solutions, although they don't need to be pre-printed. More companies are using digital printing to produce materials as needed rather than printing thousands of copies through a traditional printing process. Formatted correctly, spec sheets are easy to make accessible on your website, which makes it simple and fast for your sales team, agents, and prospects to obtain them.

Other sales support collateral options are case studies and white papers.

And lastly, don't forget business cards. Some argue they're on the decline with more people exchanging contact information electronically. That's true in some industries, but the majority of B2B companies still operate in the tangible world. Focus on high quality when purchasing business cards. It's easy to get inexpensive ones, so lots of people do. But there is a difference between high-quality business cards and the overused, standard, stock ones. It's a small thing that can make a big difference at the first impression stage.

Chapter 24—Case Studies

Case studies are a high-impact tool that allows B2B companies to demonstrate their experience and track record. A customer speaking positively on your behalf is one of the greatest sources of credibility for your company, and the ability to tell a story about actual results is much stronger than any elevator pitch.

Case studies can serve as a useful sales support tool as content on your website, as input to articles, and as the basis for speaking engagements. They can also be used as part of your lead nurturing process.

It's important to have multiple case studies. Having only one may seem questionable to potential buyers (Does that mean you only have one client? Or only one who would speak on your behalf? Have you had favourable results only once?) A single case study may be worse for your image than none. I recommend a minimum of three but five to eight is ideal. If you serve multiple industries and situations, separate the case studies into categories, so readers can easily find the case studies most relevant to them.

If you're in the enviable position of having numerous experiences that could turn into case studies, make the choice based on these factors:

a) The biggest / most impressive customer names (sanitized case studies—i.e. those where the customer can't be named—are less effective).

b) The best business results—focus on the quantifiable results of dollars ($), percentages (%), and numbers (#). Anything with those symbols catch readers' eyes and speak directly to their needs.

c) The most relevant to your marketing goals, so that your most coveted prospects will find something that will help you sell to them.

When developing a portfolio of case studies, create examples that cover the range of benefits you deliver and the range of industries you serve. Start by drawing a matrix of the industries, benefits, and results you want to showcase, and then identify potential case studies that fit into each of those categories.

How To Develop A Case Study

When embarking on your first case study, it's important to develop a framework to serve as a template for future case studies. This will save you time down the road.

Case studies typically follow a basic framework of challenge-solution-results. A successful case study layout covers eight key components:

1. A profile of the customer
2. An explanation of the challenge
3. An explanation of how your company's product/service fixed their problem
4. Clear summary of the results/ROI
5. Testimonials or quotes
6. Bold title
7. Strong visuals
8. A brief "About Us" (typically on the last page of your case study) with a link to your website where prospects can learn more.

Case studies should be one to two pages; four is acceptable if you have a lot to say and need more space for visuals and technical drawings. Any longer—unless the product / solution is particularly complex—and you will lose your audience.

It's tempting when you're writing case studies to go with the easiest customer first—the one you have the best relationship with, and the one you know will be happy to sign off on anything you develop. That's a fine way to get going. But be mindful that it isn't where you stop. Think strategically about your target market, and which customer situation is most like the customers you want to attract. It's ok to start with the easy ones, but make sure to keep going and tackle the harder—and more valuable—case study options.

In order to gather the information you need for your case study, you'll likely need to interview your client. Keep your interviews simple and structured. Send them the questions in advance, so they know what you want to cover. Here's a structure I use as a starting point (always adapt it to the specific client and situation):

Challenge
- Describe the business problem/challenge that needed to be solved.
- Have you tried to solve this problem in the past?
- What impact did this problem have on your business?

Solution
- How did you hear about our company?
- How did you decide to use our company for your solution?
- Describe the solution and how it was implemented.
- Comment on the people you worked with at our company.
- How long did it take to implement?

Results
- How did the solution help solve the problem/challenge?
- What benefits did you derive from the solution?

- What has been the measurable impact on your business from deploying this solution? (Focus on quantifiable results—$, %, #.)
- Have there been any "soft" benefits from the solution?

Make sure to capture the customer's verbatim comments during the interview so they can be turned into quotes and testimonials in the case study (and elsewhere). Once you've completed a draft, have the customer review and sign off on it.

If your client is unable to provide authorization to use their name, you can do a case that describes their industry, geography, and position in the market. It's not as credible without the client name, but it's better than no case study at all. Sometimes it is difficult or impossible for clients to sign off on case studies; larger corporations have policies that often constrain this.

Once you have a portfolio of case studies, begin integrating them into your marketing program. Feature them on your website, turn them into industry presentations or webinars, do PR around them, and use them throughout the business development process.

METRICS
- ☑ # of case studies developed
- ☑ # of views/downloads per case study (on website)

Chapter 25—White Papers and Technical Papers

White papers and technical papers are research-based documents that provide an educated opinion on a specific topic. They allow a business to take the role of trusted advisor by delivering valuable information. They are a powerful way to help establish your company as a thought leader.

A good white paper provides new insight into business issues and provides ways to address and solve them without being sales oriented. White papers educate on a particular issue and might advocate a particular type of solution, but they don't promote a particular company's solution. White papers that push a specific company or solution lose all impact and are detrimental rather than constructive in B2B marketing.

White papers and technical papers can take several approaches to educate readers: they can explain a complex issue, explore the possibilities and implications of new business innovations, share aggregated knowledge of clients' experiences, offer solutions pertaining to a particular issue or market, or introduce a company's unique insights on a topic.

Here are some guidelines for producing white papers to help establish your company as a thought leader:

- Choose a topic that aligns with your brand and is of interest to your target market. There's no point in spending the time and effort to produce a white paper, if it isn't of interest to your target market. For a list of ways to identify possible topics, see Chapter 21.

- Make the title clear and attention-grabbing. Avoid buzz words. Be slightly provocative, if that will work with your audience, for example, "The Pitfalls of Manual Time-Keeping: Making a Case for Automating" by a company that sells workforce management software or "The Top 5 Online Database Attacks and How to Stop Them" by an Internet security company. A simple, to-the-point title will attract the right readership. Numbers work well in creating intriguing titles.

- On the first page, include a brief overview describing who the paper is for and what it covers. Is it for business development managers? CEOs? Let the reader know.

- White papers take an educational approach—they include market overviews, key trends, projections on market evolution, relevant findings from third party research papers and articles, historical data, and expert advice. A well-written white paper gives readers the impression that you have proprietary expertise and are willing to share it.

- Because white papers are meant to inform, they don't mention a specific company or actively promote your business. If prospects sense that a white paper is selling to them—as opposed to providing useful expertise—it loses its value.

- White papers should be between four and fifteen pages long. Use sidebars, pull-out quotes, text boxes, and bulleted lists to emphasize key points. Including charts and graphs will support your arguments and add visual interest.

- End your white paper with a summary of implications for the reader. Including information on how the reader can use their new knowledge will help them take the next step, which may involve your company.

- Don't advertise your company in the content of the white paper, but do credit yourself at the end of the document. Include an "about" paragraph at the end of the paper with information on the author and company, including contact information.

Distributing White Papers

The next step is just as important—in fact probably more important—than creating the white paper itself. Effort must be put into promoting and distributing a white paper to see good results. I've seen many companies that almost completely wasted their efforts, because they didn't do anything with their white papers other than post them to their website.

A well-written and effective white paper should travel across hundreds of desks and inboxes in the course of its life. It can be used for months, if not years, as a marketing tool.

Ten ways to leverage your white papers:

1. Post them on your website. If they are strong white papers that share a significant amount of proprietary knowledge, consider requiring people to provide their contact information, before they can access the paper. The first time someone accesses your content, ask for just four pieces of information—first name, last name, company, and email address. If you feel very strongly about knowing who is accessing the content, email it to registrants (using the address they provided), and consider disallowing Gmail, Hotmail, and Yahoo addresses.

2. Build a separate landing page for the white paper, and optimize the page (using SEO techniques—see Chapter 33) to attract people directly to where they can download or receive it via email.

3. Do a pay-per-click campaign to promote the white paper.

4. Use the white paper as the basis for a presentation at an industry conference.

5. Use the white paper as the basis for a lunch and learn, to which you invite 20 target customers.

6. Use the white paper as the basis for a webinar, and promote it to your existing and prospective customers.

7. Write a press release about the white paper and send it to the editors of trade publications that your target audience reads.

8. Write a blog summarizing the white paper and post it to your own blog and any blogs that you are a guest author on. Be sure to include a link to the download or email page for the white paper.

9. Tweet about the white paper, update your LinkedIn and Facebook pages with a link to it.

10. Send out a link to the white paper in your regular newsletter.

METRICS
- ☑ # of white papers produced
- ☑ # of views/downloads per white paper
- ☑ # of PR mentions
- ☑ # of times prospects mention your white papers
- ☑ # of times your white papers are cited by other sources

Chapter 26—Blogs

Blogs serve two purposes in B2B marketing. They help with search engine optimization, and they demonstrate expertise. They can be a great marketing tool—but whether a blog will be great for your company depends on how well you execute it. Starting a blog is easy; maintaining an active one is more difficult. To be effective, blogs need to have fresh material—which means at least four to five new posts a month. Ideally, posts should be made regularly and frequently—about two to three per week.

That sounds easy in theory, but it is a lot of work. Assuming that a single blog post takes sixty to ninety minutes to write, keeping an active blog requires roughly three hours per week. For a senior person (and often they need to write the blogs to ensure the content is compelling), that is a substantial time commitment. If this isn't the best way to spend your marketing time, choose a different tactic.

However, if you're sure that blogging will be a good use of your marketing time, here are some tips:

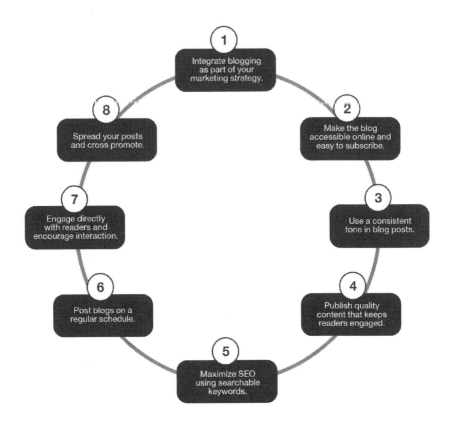

Blog Strategy

Before you commit to a blog, review your marketing strategy—your blog must be part of that strategy. You need to have a specific target audience in mind and know what kind of content that audience is interested in. Keep in mind that the vast majority of content on your blog must be relevant to your target audience and your chosen topic.

Also at this stage, decide who will write for your blog. Anyone in your company who has knowledge that is valuable to customers and prospects is an option; this includes customer service reps, consultants, engineers, technicians, marketers, and/or executives. While your blog should be maintained by the marketing division, there should always be posting opportunities for anyone who has something interesting and relevant to share. If needed, you can retain a copy editor to help clean up any blogs with rough writing.

Blog Basics

The link to your blog should be prominent on your company's website. The best way to encourage views is to host the blog on your company's webpage instead of offsite. One of the most popular blogging platforms, Wordpress, allows you to create a "blog" directory on your website and host the blog there. Make sure to include a link to your blog as part of the homepage navigation, so it's easy for visitors of your site to find your blog (and vice versa). This way, people need only search for your company name and the word "blog" to find you.

Your blog should have a clean and professional design. It's perfectly okay to start out using a blog template, but you may find it more effective to personalize a standardized template to make it reflect the general design of your website. Customizing your layout is a good way to ensure brand consistency.

Make sure that it's easy for people to subscribe to your blog. The larger your subscriber base, the more your blog becomes a way to nurture and cultivate potential customers. Distribute your content on Feedburner.com, and include buttons for users to share your posts on LinkedIn, Twitter, Facebook, and Google+.

Find Your Voice

The tone of your blog is important; the most successful corporate blogs have some personality and don't sound like they were produced by a corporation. Your company's culture will set the tone of your blog. For most companies, adopting a casual tone that's free of jargon is the best option. However, if your blog is about highly complex and technical topics for an audience of engineers, stick to a more formal writing style.

Writing a blog and finding your voice takes time and practice; give yourself a few months to get into the flow and master the art of writing posts that reflect your company's culture.

Create Quality Content

Creating strong and compelling blog posts is the most time-consuming aspect, and also the most important. Without good content, you will quickly lose readers. Keep your audience in mind at all times. Before you publish a post, look at it from the perspective of a potential customer, and ask yourself, "Did I learn something from this post? Was it of value to me?" If the answer is "no", revise your content until it delivers.

There is no single "right" way to write blogs. Inspiration can come from anywhere. It's often the day-to-day experiences, working with colleagues, and interacting with clients that yield the best blog content. You can't give away secrets, but you can usually create a phenomenal blog without revealing proprietary information.

Here are a few blog content ideas:

- Conduct interviews with industry leaders.
- Share your thoughts on industry trends and news articles.
- Create a series on a specific theme, and post it in installments; this will keep people coming back on a regular basis.
- Checked out a webinar lately? Summarize what you learned, and provide a link to it.
- Recommend a site/book/podcast that you enjoy.
- Repurpose existing marketing material content: speeches, white papers, case studies, videos, slide presentations, etc.
- Did you hear a surprising statistic the other day? Share it.
- Predict something, and defend your prediction.
- Provide write-ups on trade shows or association meetings you attended.

- Leverage customer experiences to discuss common challenges, offer suggestions, and share successes.

It's good to vary the format of blog posts. Use bullet points and numbered lists to get your points across quickly. Including photos, videos, and charts make a post eye-catching and easy to scan.

Bloggers don't need to produce all original content all the time. It's fine to act as a curator, finding and filtering great content from around the web and pointing it out in a post. Stay in the loop by subscribing to blogs on similar topics, watching for trending topics online, and engaging with other bloggers. Don't be afraid to reference content outside your blog; sharing what you know *about* is just as powerful as sharing what you know. It also gives readers insight into the business ecosystem you inhabit, which helps them understand you better.

Use Keywords

A blog will improve your search engine optimization (i.e. help your company get found online), **if** you write blogs that use your keywords. Identify the keywords that prospects use to find the services and products you provide, and make an effort in your blog to use these keywords (especially in post titles).

Be Consistent: Blog Regularly

The biggest challenge for bloggers is publishing content on a regular schedule. One trick is to stay two or three posts ahead; that way, there's a bit of a buffer if something comes up.

Find a posting schedule that works well for you and your team, and stick to it. Many blogs are started with enthusiasm and then abandoned. It's possible to stand out from the crowd simply by updating on a regular basis.

Tip: blog traffic is highest between Tuesdays and Thursdays, and blog readers are most active between 7:00am and 11:30am and after 7:00pm (when people come home from work). Posting during these times can boost your readership.

Engage With Readers

Blogs are audience-focused, which means engaging with readers is fundamental to success. After you have posted your content, readers may wish to leave comments or link to your blog. Every real comment should get a real, personalized response. It leaves a great impression for a company blog when readers' comments are being addressed. If you find your content being shared by readers somewhere else on the web, be sure to thank them; never miss an opportunity to start a dialogue or continue a discussion with readers and prospective leads.

Spread Your Content

Spreading your content is a great way to increase your subscribers. Make connections with owners of blogs on similar topics, and ask if you can guest-post for them. Contributing content to someone else's blog may seem counter-intuitive, but the results are worth the extra effort: you get exposure for your own blog and the opportunity to expand your subscriber base, and the other blogger gets the day off. If you do this, make sure your guest-post is original content—that way, you can promote your "new guest-post" on your own blog as well.

METRICS
- ☑ # of posts per month
- ☑ # of reads
- ☑ # of RSS subscribers

Chapter 27—Articles

Contributing articles to trade publications, newspapers, and online news sites is a great way to demonstrate thought leadership. Industry publications voraciously seek contributions from industry stakeholders. These outlets are often publishing one issue a month, and they rely on companies and members to provide interesting content.

Here are 8 steps for generating and submitting articles to industry publications:

Step 1: Build your List. Create a list of the 3-5 publications that have the greatest reach across your target market and create a longer list of publications that reach your audience but to a lesser extent. You can pitch some articles to the 3-5 priority publications and others to the lower priority publications.

Step 2: Review Guidelines. Identify the content submission guidelines for each publication. These are the rules you have to follow to be eligible for publication. Pick opportunities that allow you to contribute knowledge and experience to the publication and that provide your company with the greatest exposure.

Step 3: Review Editorial Calendars. Most publications develop an editorial calendar for the year. Know which upcoming issues will feature themes/trends that are closely related to your products and services.

Step 4: Review Articles from Past Issues. To get a sense of what the publication is looking for, pay attention to the tone and length of past articles and the inclusion of any supplemental material, such as images or charts.

Step 5: Develop A Process For Pitching Article Topics. Your "pitch kit" should include a brief biography of your company and the author, and 2 or 3 article ideas. Each idea should be a specific topic and include the title and key points readers will take away from it. Include previous writing samples—a few past white papers or blog posts will give the publication an idea of how well you can communicate to an audience.

Step 6: Pitch Your Article. Send your pitch kit via e-mail directly to the editor of the publication. Personalize the greeting; common courtesy goes a long way toward getting your email and attachments read.

Step 7: Pitch Again. Depending on your industry and your relationships with key media, plan to send anywhere between 3-5 pitches before one is accepted.

Step 8: Select An Author and Complete the Article. Once you've been accepted, select your author (usually the president or other senior executive) and write the complete article, customized for the publication's audience.

Once you've had your first article published, you can reap the rewards. PR has a momentum effect—once you've appeared in one publication, you're likely to get picked up by others, and possibly be asked to become a columnist for future issues.

METRICS
- ☑ # of articles pitched
- ☑ # of articles published

Chapter 28—Press Releases and Public Relations

Press releases are one of the inputs to public relations. They're a good way to boost SEO efforts and provide a regular stream of news for your audience. You can announce new products, projects, and clients, spread the word about upcoming speaking engagements or trade show appearances, and publicize other company successes. Press releases can be sent to the editors of trade publications to spark their interest and keep them apprised of progress.

Here are a few practical tips on effectively generating and distributing press releases:

1. **Write a powerful headline.** Editors have only seconds to look at a press release—if the headline doesn't grab them, they won't bother to read the rest. A good headline states the product/service and explains what is important about it (i.e. new release, major upgrade, etc). Be specific.

2. **Remember the basics.** Every press release should include the product/service name and its version number; the name, street address, phone number, and website of your company; all contact information for the person in charge of media relations; a secondary contact name and information; and the date of the product/service's availability.

3. **Focus on user benefits.** Your press release should tell readers and editors why your product or service deserves their attention. Make sure it answers, "What will this product/service do for me?" Emphasize the benefits

that readers will receive, not the features you can boast about.

4. **Use bullet points**. Readers (and especially editors) have to digest a lot of information quickly, and bullet point lists help them absorb data faster.

5. **Keep it short.** A standard press release is no more than two pages.

6. **Have a standard company description.** Create a single, benefit-focused paragraph that describes what your company actually does. For example, instead of: "SecuriCo is a leading private security company", try: "SecuriCo provides professional, private security solutions that help industrial companies protect their properties". If an editor doesn't know what your company does by the first sentence, they're not interested.

7. **Keep it time-sensitive.** Before issuing a press release for a product announcement, ensure that your company will be able to offer the product/service within the identified timeline. If you're unsure, don't send it out—a press release that promises something you can't deliver leaves a terrible impression.

8. **Post your press releases**. They can be posted very cost-effectively on sites like PRWeb, and of course, on your company's website. If you do this, make sure that you put news up regularly—there's nothing worse than visiting a website and seeing their last news update was in 2009.

9. **Send to publications.** Send press releases to relevant trade publications or directly to the editors of online sources. Make sure to follow up with a phone call—the

human touch goes a long way. See Chapter 27 on articles for more tips.

10. **Share across relevant social media channels.** Get your news out to your target market through your LinkedIn network, LinkedIn Groups, Twitter, industry blogs, Google+, and Facebook (if appropriate for your industry).

METRICS
- ☑ # of press releases developed
- ☑ # of media mentions and features

Chapter 29—Corporate Identity (some call it "brand"—mistakenly)

The words "brand" and "branding" are hot in the B2B world these days. Traditionally, it was consumer companies that focused on brand. But the appreciation of the value of a brand has crossed into B2B.

The challenge for many companies is to understand exactly what branding is. Simply put, your company's brand is its reputation. It's how customers see you—the perception they have of the company. And that perception comes from many different sources—through customers' interactions with sales reps, their use of your product, their dealings with your technical support team, etc. Brand is much bigger than any single business function—it's more than marketing, it's more than customer service, more than research and development.

For that reason, I will leave the full discussion of B2B branding to other books. What I want to tackle here is corporate identity, which is the visual representation of your business, mainly your logo and communications design. It's the Identity on your website, business card, and trade show booth.

There's a wide spectrum of B2B logos on the market. I've seen some created by world-class designers, and I've seen some designed by the fourteen-year old nephew of the company's CEO. Ultimately, a logo is not going to make or break a B2B company. For companies starting out, use one of the services like www.99designs.com to get a solid design at a great price. If your company has a logo that was designed a long time ago, it may have strong brand equity and should be changed with care. Minor tweaks are fine, but make sure it can still be recognized by your older customers.

On the other hand, there are many companies that have logos so poorly designed and outdated that even the CEO admits it's embarrassing. If this is the case, it's time for an update. This kind of project gives you an opportunity to engage with customers and employees as part of the re-design and launch process. It can be a valuable opportunity to provide company updates on progress and initiatives.

SECTION F:
ONLINE TACTICS

Chapter 30—Websites

It's hard to imagine that just ten years ago digital marketing barely existed in B2B budgets. Digital marketing is the fastest-growing marketing category; B2B marketing budgets are shifting from print, trade shows, and direct mail to digital media and more money is being added to the budget.

A good website attracts and informs prospects, generates leads, promotes the brand, and updates customers. For B2B companies, especially those who sell globally, the website is now the central pillar in marketing. It used to be that B2B companies could launch a website and forget about it for a few years. B2B buying behaviour has changed, and websites have evolved alongside it. And the pace of change is accelerating. Now website content must be kept up to date so search engines can find the site, and the appearance must be modern so that your company doesn't look antiquated.

Most small and mid-size B2B companies have updated their sites in the last five years—but many need an overhaul. It's an intensive process, so it's understandable that companies resist.

I've seen companies take months to go through the website re-development process—only to end up with a website that doesn't really serve the company. Too many businesses get caught up in the **design** of the site rather than the <u>function</u> of it. An effective website, like every B2B marketing tool, has a job to do.

As a starting point, perform an audit of your current website. Go to <u>www.marketsmartb2b.com/resources</u> for a white paper on how to conduct a website audit.

Next, consider these two questions when starting a website project:

1) Who do we want to attract to our website?
2) Once they're here, what do we want them to learn and do?

It's likely you'll have multiple answers to both questions so use a matrix to capture them. B2B purchases usually involve several stakeholders with different needs, so the information you provide has to cover all the different needs. Here's a framework I use with a high-level example.

SAMPLE: WIDGET VENDOR			
WHO DO I WANT TO ATTRACT?	**WHY ARE THEY VISITING?**	**WHAT INFO DO WE WANT THEM TO HAVE?**	**WHAT DO WE WANT THEM TO DO?**
Prospective Customers	• To learn if our widgets can improve their business	• An overview of our products (features + benefits) • A video demonstration of our product • Competitive comparison info • Customer testimonials/case studies • Purchase information (including pricing, ordering details)	• Read about our products • Watch our videos • Download a white paper/case study/article • Sign up for our newsletter • Subscribe to our blog • Contact us to set up a sales presentation
Prospective Employees	• To see what opportunities are available at our company. • To learn what the company culture is	• Company description • Job openings • Data on who works here (names, photos, etc.) How to apply; The recruiting process; The criteria	• Submit a job application

It can be helpful to review what other businesses in your industry are doing. Take a look at competitors' websites. Take notes on the ways they organize and present their information. Assess their methods, relative strengths, and weaknesses. Use this research to create your site architecture by combining their best ideas and avoiding their mistakes. Also consider other sites you've visited that have great designs. What makes them good, and can you emulate those elements?

Always Build Websites with Search Engine Optimization in Mind

Websites are no longer just information purveyors. They have to **attract** visitors to be useful. That means that when a prospect does a search for the services or products your company provides, your website needs to come up in the results.

It's vital to know the keywords that are relevant for your company and to design your website—not just the copy, but the architecture too—so that the site can be easily found. Use tools like Google AdWords' keyword tool and Hubspot to identify the keywords suited to your business.

Design Matters

While functionality is vitally important for an effective website, a good look matters too. If you haven't updated your site in a number of years, it will show—and visitors will assume your company is not current.

Here are some tips for successful website development:

1. *Hire a professional.*

   Your website is too important to entrust to a web-savvy niece or nephew or to a bargain-basement web design firm. Do a bit of research and ask peers at other companies for recommendations. Look at the "site made by" credits on websites you admire. You may not have the deepest pockets, but your company's online, visual presence is not something to skimp on.

2. *Keep your page design consistent*

A good designer will take care of this for you. Keep visitors happy and on track by having a consistent look throughout your website. Navigation menus should appear in the same place on every page. Make sure headings, font size, and typeface remain the same. Typically, websites have one layout for the homepage and one or two additional layouts (no more) for the internal pages.

3. *Keep the website mobile-friendly*

More and more business people are viewing websites on their smartphones, netbooks, and tablet computers. These devices are limited in what they can display—for example, iPads are infamous for not allowing Adobe Flash content—so avoid using a layout that runs the risk of complicating a mobile users' browsing experience.

4. *Keep the site lean and fast*

Internet surfers have short attention spans, so your website needs to load fast to stop viewers from clicking away. If the site takes more than five seconds to load, not many people will stick around to see it.

5. *Use A Content Management System (CMS)*

A CMS is a type of software hosted on your website that makes it easy to edit webpages. Not only does it make website maintenance simple for the average user, but it is especially useful for complex websites with many pages. It makes it easier for multiple people to manage the site.

Like most aspects of website development, a CMS takes some technical effort to get up and running, so you're better off having your web design firm do the initial work. But once it's implemented, you can maintain your website through the CMS rather than having to call your web developer to add every new press release and product update.

6. *Plan ahead*

The design and programming platform should take into account future website additions, such as new sections, pages, or functionalities. Plan now to avoid high costs in the future.

Buyer-Focused Content

Design your site with buyers in mind—after all, they *are* the type of visitors you're trying to attract. Too often, companies get caught up in the bells and whistles of website design and neglect the fundamental function of a website: communicating your message to buyers.

Buyers search on the Internet and visit company sites, because they are looking for solutions. They have a time-sensitive agenda with little room for aimless exploring. While different types of buyers have different needs, all buyers want to work with companies who "get" them. They are more apt to investigate websites that speak directly to their unique situation, challenges, and goals. The tone of your copy plays a big part in this.

Calls to Action

Once a buyer has visited your website and determined that they are interested in what you offer, they want to know what to do next. This is why every webpage needs a call to action—a box, button, or link that says "do this now!"

A standard "telephone us for more information" button is a basic necessity. A more effective call to action is customized to that exact page or to a targeted need. Specific actions like "call to arrange a sales presentation" or "click here to register for our webinar" will lead prospects in the right direction.

Sign-Up Forms

Much like calls to action, every page of your website should feature an invitation for visitors to become prospects. It is possible to gather valuable information about who is visiting your site by asking for a few basic details before visitors can access certain types of high-level content.

For example, introductory information, such as product listings and data sheets, may be freely accessible. More complex content, such as technical specifications or proprietary white papers, may merit registration. Ask only for the basic information—first name, last name, company, and email.

Share Buttons

Are your pages easy for users to share? Every page should have embedded widgets that enable readers to e-mail, bookmark, Tweet, Google+1, or Facebook "Like" your page. These buttons typically appear at the bottom of the content and are simple to add to a template.

Downloadable Content

Downloadable documents are vital for B2B company websites, but your existing print media may be difficult to transfer online. The solution to this is two-fold: first, convert existing print collateral into a digital format and second, ensure that all future marketing collateral is designed with both print and web in mind.

The best way to make your print material web friendly is to convert it to PDF files using Adobe Acrobat®. PDF files are standard on the web, and almost every computer has a PDF reader (such as Adobe Reader or Foxit Reader) that allows users to view and print documents. To create a PDF, all you need is the original files: Adobe® Acrobat® can make PDFs from files created in design and layout programs, as well as any documents created with Microsoft® Word or other word processing programs.

See the article on creating SEO-friendly PDFs on www.marketsmartb2b.com/resources.

When designing marketing collateral, adhere to some basic guidelines to make sure they work well both online and offline:

- The page size should be letter size (8.5"x11"). This will allow the documents to be easily printed by almost any office printer.

- Printed sales and technical sheets are often double-sided, but this doesn't work on the web—create an alternative, web-friendly design that naturally breaks into individual 8.5"x11" pages.

- Most users print PDFs in black and white, so optimize your documents accordingly. When picking colours, avoid using shades that will blend together if converted to greyscale. Avoid white text on dark backgrounds—not only is this hard to read on screen, but it wastes a lot of ink when printed.

- If you include photographs or images, have both low-resolution and high-resolution versions on hand. High-resolution images are required for commercial printing, but they can lead to oversized PDF files that will take customers a long time to download and open. Lower quality graphics work better on screen and for individual printing.

While it's important to have these documents available for download, PDFs should never take the place of web pages.

Ideally, the information in your PDF should also be available for users who would prefer to read the website only.

METRICS

- ☑ # of unique visitors
- ☑ Average # of page views
- ☑ Top search terms that bring people to your website
- ☑ Length of time visitors spend on each page
- ☑ Bounce rate

The most popular tool to measure website performance is Google Analytics. It's free, relatively easy to use, and on par with expensive analytics programs available for purchase.

Chapter 31—Microsites

If your company has multiple product lines or brands, you may want to use microsites—websites within a website—to focus on one specific aspect of your business.

Microsites benefit both the company and the user. B2B buyers save time, because they don't have to wade through numerous pages to get to the content they need, and microsites allow them to share relevant content with their fellow purchasers quickly and easily. And as the microsite provider, you can capture more valuable, targeted leads and develop more thorough buyer profiles.

It's popular to build a microsite around the launch of a new product or an event you're hosting. Think of the microsite as a product information packet or a glossy sell sheet created to complement and supplement the information on your corporate website.

Chapter 32—Landing Pages

A landing page is a single webpage hosted on your site that catches visitors who arrive from search engines, e-mails, or ads and converts them into prospects. Landing pages focus on a single topic and many can be built from the same, basic template. They are cost-effective, quick to produce, and can turn anonymous web visitors into valuable prospects.

Whether your landing page offers a white paper, collects event sign-ups, or provides other valuable content, the main goal of the page is to get the visitor to accept your offer.

Software like Hubspot makes it easy for companies to create landing pages. You can also hire a web development company to create one for you. You can then replicate it yourself for future landing pages.

Follow these tips to optimize landing pages and deliver a strong, clear message that encourages visitors to take the next step:

- **Brand Your Landing Page**
  Your company name and logo should be prominent on the landing page, so visitors know what site they are on.

- **Be Consistent: Match Your Landing Page With Your Ad**
  Industry professionals click ads that interest them in order to learn more, so be sure that your landing page matches the ad and adheres to your brand guidelines. Repeat your offer by using the same text, graphics, and colours. This will reassure visitors that they've clicked to the right place.

- **Have a Good Headline**
  The headline of the landing page is the first thing visitors will read, and it's also the key element for SEO. You want to make it as memorable and attention-grabbing as possible, In as little words as possible. Write (and re-write!) your headline until it is search engine optimized and is a direct, brief, benefit-oriented statement that tells visitors why they need what you're offering.

- **Create and Repeat Your Call-To-Action**
  Create a clear call-to-action and give it prime positioning at the top of the landing page. "Download Now" or "Register Today" are powerful words that can inspire action; pair these action words with an appropriate, clickable graphic. Make sure to repeat the call-to-action as text and button links throughout the page.

- **Keep the Copy Simple**
  Write only as much copy as necessary to communicate your value proposition—then stop. Get straight to the point by keeping your copy focused on the benefits of accepting your offer. Use short sentences and paragraphs, and take advantage of bold headlines and bullet points that allow people to skim your content and get to your call-to-action faster. Graphics, when used sparingly, are effective.

- **Remove Navigation Temptations**
  A landing page is not a full website; it's a single page focused purely on lead conversion. Don't run the risk of letting prospects wander away from your offer—eliminate any distractions that could encourage visitors to click around your main website and lose sight of their original intent.

- **Embrace White Space**
  How can you expect visitors to focus on your offer if they're overwhelmed by too many graphics and too

much text? Landing pages should be clean and open with big fonts and plenty of white space. Less is more.

Keep all key information "above the fold"—the part of the screen that users can see without scrolling. Browsersize from Google Labs (http://browsersize. googlelabs.com) is a free tool that can help.

In addition, try a two-column page layout. Layouts with a main column and a narrow, second column have the highest conversion rates. Use the main column to convey your offer and primary value proposition and the narrow column to repeat key points and link to the offer.

- **Simplify Forms**
  Long sign-up forms with many required fields hurt conversion rates. Keep forms simple and uncomplicated to encourage participation. A prospect's name, company, and email address is all you need at this stage; the rest of their information can be gathered later as you engage with them and learn more about them, their business, and their needs.

- **Engage With New Leads Right Away**
  Respond as soon as possible to all leads generated through your landing pages. These visitors have entrusted you with their contact information, so show them you appreciate their visit by quickly engaging with them. Once a prospect has filled out your form, have the landing page redirect them to a page that confirms their submission and thanks them for their time and information. For the follow-up email, set up an automated response system that sends out a message to thank the prospect for accepting your offer. The email should also provide links to other information about your company. Now that you've captured the lead, you can give them more content options.

- **Never Stop Testing**
  Even if you're getting great results from your landing pages, there's always room for improvement. Keep testing variations to compare results—experiment by placing the call-to-action in different places, using different words and headlines, or using different page layouts. Change only one aspect at a time, and track its impact on conversion rates. Alternatively, use A/B testing—have two different variations of your landing page, and measure which version (Version A or Version B) is most successful. Keep any changes that increase conversions, and apply this knowledge to other landing pages for other campaigns.

METRICS
- ☑ The search terms that bring people to your landing page
- ☑ # of views
- ☑ # of downloads

Chapter 33—Search Engine Optimization (SEO) and Pay Per Click (PPC)

Search engine optimization is the process of getting your website ranked as highly as possible in search engine results through the use of keywords. This is known as the "organic" method. On the other hand, "pay-per-click" (PPC) are ads displayed by search engines that link to your website. You only have to pay when people click on them. The most popular PPC provider is Google Adwords. LinkedIn advertising is also growing in popularity among B2B companies.

Is SEO or PPC more effective? Which is easier? Which is faster? There are compelling points for and against each. Any marketer who has the budget and resources should use both for their different strengths and the benefits that can be achieved by leveraging them together.

Keywords and key phrases are the way to improve search engine optimization. If you're not sure how they work, check out Google's Keyword Tool—a free way to help you choose which keywords your SEO campaign should focus on. Entering your company URL and clicking "search" will show you a list of Google-suggested phrases, their popularity, and how many times they are searched for. The Google Keyword Tool will also help you identify related terms, compare the demand between different keywords, and help you find new phrases and keywords you may benefit from using.

Your website is only useful if your target market can find it. While some of your visitors may type in your company URL, many more will find your company via Google or another major search engine. It's your job to make sure that your website ranks near the top in searches related to your business.

Having a good SEO program can propel your listing from page ten to page one. There are many firms that do SEO exclusively and can help you improve your results. If you're lean on budget, the basics of SEO aren't hard to learn. The harder part is patience: it can take anywhere from three to six months to see results from your SEO efforts. And constant maintenance of your program is essential to success—SEO is never "done".

Some tips on D.I.Y SEO:

1. *Index your site on Google*—This sounds simplistic, but it's always wise to double-check that your web vendor has indexed your site on Google. If not, a quick visit to http://www.google.com/addurl/?continue=/addurl should fix that.

2. *Page Titles*—Every page on your website should have a unique page title; avoid generic names, such as "About" or "Home Page". The titles should include the most important keyword phrase(s) used on the page and be no longer than sixty-five characters.

3. *Meta Description*—A meta description is a few sentences of text embedded into the code of each web page that search engines display when your site is listed in results. Your website's meta description should be a few short sentences that describe your company and what it does.

    ("Meta descriptions" are the main type of meta tags used for SEO. They are often confused with "meta keyword" tags, which are useless. Years ago, search engines used websites' meta keywords (lists of keywords embedded into the website code) to rank results. But because this made it easy for unscrupulous people to game the system by stuffing their pages with hundreds of popular keywords, search engines stopped paying attention to them.)

4. *Document Titles*—Every downloadable document on your website should have a proper file name. Include your company's name, the document's title, and use hyphens instead of spaces.

5. *Tagged Images/Videos*—Make sure each of your graphics and videos is tagged and captioned (these are commonly referred to as "alt tags"). This makes it easier for search engines to pick up on keywords and include your rich content in results.

6. *Keyword Rich Content*—Every page of your website should consist of strategic and appropriate keyword rich content. Don't fill a page with lots of keywords just for the sake of having them; ensure it is done in a natural way. Google suggest that your content should have 1-2% keywords. If terminology changes in your industry or new trends emerge, edit your content to reflect those changes to help drive traffic to your site.

Keeping your website search engine optimized can be laborious. If you don't feel comfortable with DIY SEO, consider hiring a professional. An SEO firm will charge anywhere from $500 to $5,000 per month—but you'll have a strong partner to help you monitor changes in keyword traffic and usage, and to adapt your link building and on-page optimization efforts.

International SEO

North America is a Google-centric world. While Bing (Microsoft's search engine) is gaining market share, Google still has the majority of the search market.

But if you're selling and marketing your products and services internationally, it's important to know that Google isn't the only game in town. Any investment you make in search engine optimization must be tailored to the markets you're targeting.

Some markets and search engines to consider:

- *China:* Baidu owns the vast majority of the market, and Google has declined because of the public spat over censorship between the company and the Chinese government.

- *Russia:* Yandex is the leader with about two-thirds of the market, and Google trails significantly behind.

- *South Korea:* Naver has more than two-thirds of the market. Google is almost non-existent.

- *Japan:* Yahoo!/Bing lead with almost half the market.

- *Czech Republic*: Seznam.cz owns over half the market.

If you work with an SEO company, make sure they have experience dealing with these other search engines and that they're optimizing your site to perform well on them. Most SEO companies focus on Google, but if you're trying to grow in Russia, you're missing 75% of that market.

Pay-Per-Click (PPC)

With PPC, you bid on specific search terms and phrases that you want your ad to appear alongside in results. Ads appear in the highlighted section at the top and right side of the Google results page.

PPC ads are ranked by often they are clicked and on the relevance of the linked page to your ad. It doesn't matter how much you bid for a keyword; if your ad fails to connect with users, and Google doesn't think the linked page matches your ad closely enough, your ad will slip to the bottom of the PPC pile.

An ad must be the answer to the searcher's question. A PPC and its accompanying landing page should be created along the same lines as an organic search "meta description" snippet and its landing page.

Design your PPC ads with this in mind. Use it to offer something to your audience—a white paper, webinar, or demo—that will compel searchers to click your ad and visit your website; action words work well here.

If you can't get your ad to the top of the list, don't worry. While the top slot will almost always receive a higher volume of traffic, some of that traffic may be "impulse clicks" that lower the overall quality. It's better to have lower volume with higher quality—users who are more motivated to buy and more likely to convert—which can still be achieved with a low PPC ranking.

A useful aspect of PPC that is often overlooked is the ability to use negative keywords to specify which words you *do not* want your ad associated with. Filtering out unqualified traffic will help you avoid spending money for clicks that don't convert to leads. Your negative keywords will depend on what industry you're in, but here are some starter recommendations: *freeware*, *bargain*, *cheap*, *salaries*, *public domain*, *lawsuits*, and *consumer.*

METRICS
- ☑ Clicks per budget
- ☑ # of downloads through PPC

Chapter 34—Email Marketing

Email marketing offers short turn-around time and quick delivery while remaining cost-effective. A solid email strategy can build your brand and foster relationships with customers. It is among the most effective B2B marketing tools.

The challenge for B2B companies today is to get their messages through to the inboxes of customers and prospects. It's increasingly complex to navigate the legislation that governs email communications. Here are some tips to help you achieve effective email marketing:

Know the law. Find out the regulations on email marketing in your jurisdiction. If you prefer, hire a professional who knows the law and can ensure you stay compliant.

Identify yourself. Be sure that a name familiar to your potential consumers appears in the email's "From" line. Emails from unknown and unidentified addresses are much more likely to be deleted.

Use compelling subject lines. Your email's subject line is the headline; keep it short, attention-grabbing, and benefit-oriented. The subject line has the highest impact on whether your message gets read, so it's worth spending time on. Keep your subject line under forty characters to ensure it won't get cut off.

Keep important content in the preview pane. The majority of B2B email readers use a preview pane before opening emails. Design your messages with this in mind; put the most important content (your key selling benefits and the offer) and a call to action in the top 300-500 pixels of your email. Don't waste space with an oversize logo or header—use the format to your best advantage.

Provide relevant content. The most important thing you should do is provide content that is so interesting and relevant to your readers that they look forward to receiving every email you send. Your content should help them do their jobs: how-to articles, best practices guidelines, mini-case studies, and application ideas are effective email content.

Use images carefully. Images add visual interest and relevance to your emails; thumbnails of white paper covers and product images are a good way to introduce graphics that will not distract from your content. But be wary of making your emails too reliant on images, many B2B users disable images in their email programs.

Write focused copy. Know the purpose of your message and the action(s) you want readers to take *before* you compose your email, and then write your copy with those key goals in mind. Use bold headlines, short paragraphs and sentences, and bullet points. Don't include lengthy articles that force the reader to scroll: instead, offer brief summaries and provide a URL for readers to view the full article. This approach allows you to track which articles generate the most clicks—telling you what readers are interested in.

Measure and test. Track the key metrics of the emails you send—open rate, click-through rate, conversion rate—and test new ways to improve results. A good benchmark to start with is 15-20% open rate with a 4-5% click-through. An easy way to test a single change is by creating two different versions of the email and sending each version to half your mailing list.

This "A/B" testing will help you make specific changes and continually improve.

Never use Outlook to send your e-newsletter, unless you have less than ten recipients. There are good, cost-effective, online tools that will help you stay compliant with legislation. They'll also help you track the performance of your marketing. Some of the most popular email marketing services are Constant Contact (http://www.constantcontact.com) and MailChimp (http://www.mailchimp.com).

When to Send

There is much debate over the best time to send B2B emails. In my experience, the most effective time is Tuesday to Thursday afternoon around 3 to 4 pm. Monday mornings are when people are busy preparing for the week, so their immediate tasks take priority over your emails, whereas during mid-week afternoons, they are more likely to take the time to go through their inbox.

METRICS
- ☑ Click-through rate
- ☑ Open rate
- ☑ # of subscribers
- ☑ Total # of unsubscribes
- ☑ # SPAM complaints

Chapter 35—Video

I predict that within three years, every B2B website will utilize video. Why? It's partly because people are lazy and find it easier to watch a video than to read. But mostly it's because video is versatile and can be used for many functions. Video is especially useful for B2B companies, because it enables a lot of technical information to be covered quickly.

Creating video for your website isn't as difficult as it was ten years ago. Today, by using the basic software and hardware built into most standard computers, you can create simple, informative videos. They don't have to be fancy—just look into the camera and talk. Alternatively, you can edit together footage demonstrating your work or how you solved a problem.

You can worry less about production quality than in the past. In most cases, all you need is a well-lit segment with a basic, digital video camera and decent audio quality.

Keep videos short: staying around one to two minutes will help keep your audiences' attention and help you stay focused on a single theme.

Using video to demonstrate B2B products is powerful. A short product overview gives your customers and prospects a much better understanding of your product, because they are able to see it in its natural setting; it improves conversion rates, because video is still considered impressive, and it saves your business development and technical teams a lot of time explaining, demonstrating, and reviewing your products to prospects.

Don't forget about video blogging and video case studies as well, and consider creating a YouTube channel where all your videos can live.

YouTube

YouTube.com is the #1 video-sharing site and the #2 search engine—surpassed only by parent company Google. Its ease of use and near worldwide accessibility make it an ideal way to share your videos with prospects globally.

To make good use of YouTube, create a channel for your company and post all videos there. Include keyword rich descriptions for each video to allow them to be easily found and always include links back to your website.

METRICS
- ☑ # of videos created
- ☑ # of views
- ☑ Amount of viewing time (did viewers watch the whole thing?)

Chapter 36—Webinars

Webinars are online seminars offered live to participants, and then later available for download. They are relatively new digital tools. They hold a lot of promise but take a lot of work and need the right situation to deliver strong results. Some B2B companies use webinars to great effect—but often, despite great effort, they don't generate the desired results.

To use webinars effectively, you need a list of about 500 people to invite. F the content is a good match for invitees, you'll get about a 10% uptake, i.e. 50 people will sign up. Of those who sign up, roughly half will actually attend.

Like all B2B marketing, the event itself will not deliver all the value—it's the before and after activities that do. Before the webinar, you should promote the event to your existing customer base (if it's relevant for them), your prospect list, and any other group—it's great to partner with an industry association to promote the webinar to their membership.

Start promoting the webinar—three to four weeks in advance, and send reminders one week ahead and one day ahead. When someone registers, send an acknowledgment email and a calendar invitation, so the time will be held in their calendar.

Following the webinar, post the archived session on your website (this is valuable content, so consider requiring registration to access it).

Send a follow-up to those who attended and provide ways for them to continue to engage with you—invite them to an upcoming local event, suggest an in-person meeting, or simply ask if they want to receive your regular newsletter. The point is to find a way to nurture the relationship.

METRICS
- ☑ # of attendees
- ☑ # of downloads
- ☑ # of follow ups
- ☑ # of leads

Chapter 37—Lead Nurturing Systems (Marketing Automation)

A major innovation in B2B marketing over the last five years has been the move towards lead nurturing. Lead nurturing is the idea that B2B prospects may engage with a company at various stages of the purchase process. They may be researching and a long way from purchasing, or they may be ready to make a purchase in the next week. Lead nurturing, also called marketing automation, is a process that allows the marketing team to nurture leads that aren't yet ready for an interaction with the sales team. The objective of lead nurturing is to build the prospect's knowledge of and trust in your company, so that when they're ready to buy, they buy from you.

Lead nurturing systems allow companies to nurture leads in a consistent, well-structured, and cost effective way. When well implemented and managed, they are more reliable and effective than nurturing left to the sales team.

The first step in lead nurturing is to identify who you are nurturing and what messages you want to convey. If you've completed the marketing strategy process in Part One, you already have this information—you know your target market(s), your value proposition, and your messaging.

The next step is to design your nurturing process. How do you want to communicate to your leads, with what content, and when? The core of lead nurturing is a solid plan. Lead nurturing systems allow you to program a set of email communications to go out to prospects at set intervals or on a particular calendar.

You can also intersperse calls from the sales team to add another dimension to your lead nurturing process.

When a lead is first engaging with your company, it's important to confirm that they want to receive communications from you in the future—the laws are getting more stringent about this (see Chapter 34—Email Marketing). Once you have permission to communicate with a lead, you're able to send them email updates on product innovations, new installations, and invitations to webinars and other events. The key to effective lead nurturing is content. A good program will need ten to fifteen pieces of content (e-books, white papers, articles, case studies, etc.) to send to prospects. The system will indicate who is opening which emails, so you can see what content is most compelling to prospects and also which prospects are most engaged with you. Lead nurturing allows you to intensify your communication with those who appear closer to a purchase decision than others—for example, if a lead has opened and read all of your newsletters and attended the webinar you held last week, they're likely more qualified for a sales call than a lead who hasn't opened your last three newsletters.

There are a growing number of lead nurturing/marketing automation systems. They vary in their strengths and weaknesses. For small and mid-size B2B companies, the most popular systems are:

- Marketo (Spark Edition)
- Hubspot
- Silverpop
- Infusionsoft

If you'd like an outline to help you set up your lead nurturing program, download one at www.marketsmartb2b.com.

Chapter 38—Social Media
(LinkedIn, Twitter, and Facebook)

B2B relationships are fundamentally about people, so it makes sense that B2B marketing is increasingly done through social media. This is a shift occurring at different speeds in different industries and segments. The pace of change is accelerating, and even the least digitally savvy industries are now moving towards social media. Many B2B companies are intrigued but remain unsure—where does it fit for their organization, and where should they start? In this chapter, I'll cover the most relevant social media tools for B2B companies and how to use them.

There are two important things for B2B companies to understand about social media. First, it's about having a dialogue, not a dictation, with customers and prospects. Second, it's resource intensive. It takes more than just an hour or two here and there for it to result in traction for your company.

Below are the three most important social media sites in order of importance for B2B companies: LinkedIn, Twitter, and Facebook. Each social media site has distinct applications for B2B marketing.

- Job-hunting, networking, recruiting
- Strengthen business relationships
- Assert thought leadership in industry

- Assert thought leadership in industry
- Increase company's Google hits
- Disseminate information or provoke conversation with customers and industry

facebook.

- Engage with customers/prospects via Fan Page
- Can have limited applications for most B2B industries

LinkedIn

LinkedIn.com is the world's largest online, professional social network with about 200 million members in over 200 countries and territories.

LinkedIn's most important feature is "connections", a way of mapping members together based on their common contacts—it's like an online version of "six degrees of separation". Because members may only directly message their primary contacts, networking happens via arranged introductions or through LinkedIn's suggested contacts; this ensures that all networking is kept professional and done through trusted channels.

As a tool for professional networking, job-hunting, and recruiting, LinkedIn is fantastic. Having a company presence on the site can help you develop and strengthen business relationships, stay up to date on industry information, demonstrate thought leadership in your niche, and increase search traffic for your company website.

Here are some tips on using LinkedIn in your B2B marketing:

Personal Profiles

All management, business development, marketing, and customer facing employees at your company should have a personal profile on LinkedIn.

1. <u>Keep your company name in their headline.</u> The default for the headline field is the member's position at their current company.

2. <u>Use a professional photo.</u> Every social network profile needs a photo, so if your company has team photos—especially ones with a distinctive style or background—this is the perfect place to use them. It isn't essential that the photo be shot with the company logo in the background or even that it is a standard, corporate headshot, but it should be something reasonably professional.

3. <u>Link to your company website.</u> Change the default link category from "My Website" to "Other" in order to have a customizable field to enter the company name and your website or blog URL. This creates a better anchor link to connect traffic from your website to LinkedIn.

4. <u>Use a keyword rich summary.</u> Although many users fill the "Summary" section with personal information, make sure that employee profile summaries include company keywords. This will help Google and LinkedIn searchers discover both the employee and your company.

5. <u>Follow the company.</u> The more people (including employees) who click "follow company" on your company page, the more connected your page becomes.

Set Up a Company Page

A company page provides B2B companies with a listing that can be useful for staff recruiting and customer acquisition:

1. **Overview:** This main page features basic information about your company (i.e.: location, industry, number of employees), information about employees, content from your connected Twitter/blog feeds, and a "follow company" feature that lets other users subscribe to your page for updates.

2. **Careers:** The careers page features job postings that can be customized to target particular audiences depending on your LinkedIn membership level.

3. **Analytics** (Private): This is a private tab, accessible only to LinkedIn users who have administrator access to your company page. This page includes the number of page views, unique visitors, and clicks per month on each link of your "Products & Services" tab. It also provides the number of followers per month sorted by industry, function, and company.

LinkedIn Groups

Groups are a great B2B marketing resource. They are designed for people with similar interests to connect. There are groups for almost every professional industry and discussions are serious, focused, and active.

You can join up to fifty groups, but it's best to limit yourself to the number you can really focus on. Pick groups that represent your target market or that are good professional resources for you. Check in on your groups a few times per week and try to participate as often as possible. Replying to previous comments, sharing your thoughts or insight on a topic, and asking thought provoking questions will help add value to discussions.

Once you have a feel for what makes a popular post, you can start your own discussion—ask a question, solicit advice, or post a relevant or interesting article or resource for the group's benefit.

If the discussions you start prove popular with other group members, you may be recognized as "Top Influencer" in the group page sidebar. This recognition can help you build trust within the group. And as long as your personal profile is company based, everyone will know what you do without you having to consciously market yourself.

A caveat on LinkedIn—it does have a downside. Recruiters are very active on LinkedIn, and by making employees' information widely available, you are allowing the possibility that they will be approached to take work opportunities elsewhere. This may not be an issue in your organization—but I've seen situations in which updating an employee's LinkedIn profile was the first step on their road to leaving a company.

Twitter

Twitter is a micro-blogging site that has exploded in popularity and now has over 100 million active users. It is particularly popular with professionals in the technology, marketing, and communication fields. Twitter's unique feature is that it allows communications of only 140 characters or less.

Twitter helps increase a company's presence on Google, because tweets are now searchable in real time and appear in search results. Beyond enhancing SEO, the key question for B2B companies considering Twitter is this: are your customers or their influencers on Twitter? If not, don't worry about it, Twitter will not be a productive marketing tool. If they are, Twitter can be a great tool—if you use it well.

If you decide to use Twitter in your marketing, start by outlining your goals. Do you want to use it to promote yourself and your content to your target audience, or do you want to engage in conversations with your audience and try to build relationships? The two are different and require different time commitments.

Tweeting to inform means that you're tweeting blog posts, press releases, opinions, newsworthy articles, sales promotions, industry relevant resources, trade show reports, and the like. This is all content that may be of genuine interest to your existing customers and prospects. People follow companies on Twitter to educate themselves and keep up to date on the latest industry trends.

The informational Twitter strategy is straightforward—the tricky part is having the valuable, interesting content to tweet about. There's too much traffic on Twitter for meaningless tweets to gain an audience. Before you blast out a tweet, make sure it contains content that will reflect positively on you and your brand.

The other approach to Twitter is conversational, in which the goal is interaction with your audience. This is a more personal approach that helps humanize your company, which in turn makes people more interested in re-tweeting you, advocating your brand, and—most importantly—doing business with you.

This approach requires more time and effort than the "tweet it and leave it" informative strategy. This method requires that your Twitter identity is a personal face—because people would prefer to talk with some*one*, not some*thing*—as well as a primary account monitor who is constantly online and able to participate in real time. This exclusively personal approach works well if you or another individual in the company is interested in and able to be the Twitter go-to. They have to fully commit to being active—very active—on Twitter.

No matter which strategy you use, make sure that your tweets are useful, interesting, and compelling to your target audience. The goal is for your Twitter community to do something—ask for more information, arrange a meeting, place an order, or otherwise engage with you.

Tweeting Tools

Most serious Twitter users have turned to alternative interfaces to tweet, send direct messages, and organize their followers—and these outside programs also offer additional features, such as the ability to schedule tweets in advance, tweet from multiple accounts, and track specific hashtags and conversations.

HootSuite (www.hootsuite.com) is a web based platform that adds incredible functionality to tweeting whether you choose the free or premium versions. Another option is Tweetdeck (www.tweetdeck.com).

Facebook

Facebook hardly needs an introduction—it's the de facto social networking site, moving towards one billion users around the globe.

But can this powerful social networking tool help you market your business? Yes—but only to a certain degree. Facebook will be a major resource for B2B companies to market themselves, but it's not there yet for most B2B industries.

While not many small and mid-size B2B companies are using Facebook as a primary marketing or business development function, I suggest setting up a "Fan Page" for your company and using it to engage with customers and prospects. Setting this up is easy thanks to the "Facebook For Business" resource centre (https://www.facebook.com/business). This microsite offers clear instructions for creating and managing pages as well as additional information on Facebook ads, Sponsored Stories, and applications.

The pages section is where you should dedicate your Facebook marketing resources. Their five, simple steps to building a page are worth following and be sure to pay attention to the additional step of a conversation calendar that will help you plan your content updates.

METRICS
- ☑ Website traffic, SEO rankings, # of visitors or hits
- ☑ # of leads/sales sourced directly from social media
- ☑ # of social media followers/"Fans"
- ☑ Mentions in social media
- ☑ # of unique website visitors referred by social media

Chapter 39—Online Reputation Monitoring

There are good online tools for keeping abreast of industry trends and competitor movement as well as coverage of your own company. Keeping a close eye on how your market and areas of expertise are mentioned online can be a valuable way to spot trends, avoid negative press, and capitalize on positive mentions.

The easiest tool is Google Alerts (http://www.google.com/alerts). Google Alerts is a free but powerful tool that sends alerts as they happen, once a day, or weekly based on specified keywords. Anyone can request keyword alerts: simply enter in the keywords you want to monitor, select how frequently you want to be alerted, what type of content you want to include (news sites, blogs, discussion forums, videos, etc.) and your email address. You'll receive an email to confirm the alert and after confirmation, alerts will begin arriving in your Inbox. The advantage of Google Alerts is that it pushes information to you rather than you having to seek it out.

There are also more sophisticated tools like Radian6 that are useful for companies that have a significant online presence and need constant monitoring.

SECTION G:
OFFLINE TACTICS

Chapter 40—Executive Seminars and Lunch and Learns

Executive seminars, as well as Lunch and Learns, are very effective B2B marketing tactics when your company has expertise to share. You host an informational event for a small group of prospects at their location, yours, or a convenient meeting venue. The events are low pressure, offer valuable information to both sides, and create a good impression of your company in your prospects' minds.

Getting the right audience for your seminar is the hardest part—you don't want the majority of your audience to be competitors and job-seekers. When considering if events can work for you, think carefully about your target audience. Are they the kind of people who will go to external or internal events? If you are pitching CEOs, is it likely they'll come to a breakfast seminar that you're offering? Is the topic that you're covering so hot and your expertise so compelling that they will seek you out at 7:00am on a cold winter morning? I find companies can be overly optimistic about prospects' interest levels.

If you decide you can make seminars work, here are some tips to success:

Choose a convenient venue and date. Think about your target audience—what is a convenient location for them? They're not going to drive an hour to attend your breakfast seminar. They probably won't drive downtown if their office is in the suburbs. Your venue doesn't need to be fancy; it needs to convey an appropriate image of your company (I once attended a seminar for an accounting firm in a log cabin, it was bizarre). They can also be held at the site of your clients, prospects, or influencers. They're particularly popular at consulting engineering firms.

Host on a Tuesday, Wednesday, or Thursday morning. July, August, and December are usually bad times because people are on holidays. January and February may present difficult weather depending on your region. Conversely, March through April and September through November can be very busy with trade shows and other events.

Create a microsite to promote the event. Do this if your event is open. If the event is closed (i.e. for employees of just one company, such as a lunch and learn at a consulting engineering firm) you do not need a microsite. A microsite allows you to easily promote the event through all outgoing communications (email signatures, newsletters, email campaigns, etc).

Promote the event. For open events, post the event on your homepage, send out invitations to your current customers and full prospects database, hand out invitations at events up to a month ahead of time, tweet about it, include it in your email signature, distribute a press release to editors of relevant publications, and post it to online sites (such as Chambers of Commerce). Be creative in spreading the word.

Make registration easy. Use a service like EventBrite (www. eventbrite.com) to make registering for the event hassle free.

If you're using the event as a lead generation tool and are hosting it independently, don't charge a fee. Only 50% of your registrants will show up on the day of the event, but if you're hoping to attract potential customers, you'll do better in the end if you don't charge people to attend.

If you're doing the event in partnership with an industry association, board of trade, or other group, you are more likely to be able to charge—but keep the fee under fifty dollars unless you're doing a long event with significant learning opportunities for the attendees.

Provide food. Make it clear on the invitation what you're providing. If attendees arrive expecting dinner, and all you have planned is canapés, you're going to have a grumpy crowd.

Encourage audience participation early. There's nothing worse than a lecture that drones on and on. I personally don't like the cheesy games and giveaways that some speakers do at the start of presentations, but I've seen even serious crowds (medical specialists) respond positively to a pop quiz with prizes thrown into the crowd. Do whatever fits the presenter's personality.

Include a question and answer session. This is a great way to interact with attendees and get them interested in what you have to offer. You have to be very familiar with the subject matter to be effective in Q & A. If you do, this is the section where you're most likely to gain traction with the audience. If you don't know the subject matter cold, limit the amount of Q & A as it can do more damage than good.

Leave them wanting more. Don't give away all your knowledge. The true objective of this kind of session is to share some expertise and convey the complexity of the problem you solve (i.e. it isn't easy for attendees to solve it on their own). Encourage attendees to engage with you for more discussion following the event. If they leave with everything they need to do the job themselves, you've defeated the purpose of holding the event.

Nurture the leads. Once the event is over, communicate with the leads you gained. Follow up with them as soon as possible and begin the lead nurturing process with an easy and appropriate next step.

METRICS
- ☑ # of attendees
- ☑ # of leads
- ☑ # of follow-up meetings

Chapter 41—Trade Shows

Trade shows are still the most commonly used B2B marketing tactic with over 90% of B2B companies utilizing them according to a 2011 study by Marketing Sherpa.

However, in recent years, the popularity and ROI of trade shows has declined. Instead of attending three or four big name shows and a couple of mid-size ones each year, companies are shifting towards smaller, regional shows or one large show. B2B companies are more likely to prioritize one or two big shows in combination with a number of local ones and to cut out the midsize shows all together.

Typically, the large shows are valuable for building brand and generating a large number of leads. These shows are very expensive, so if a company is going to pursue them, they need to have the right position in the market to leverage the opportunity (i.e. have enough money to spend to make their presence known), and the structure and processes to follow up effectively with leads after the show.

Smaller, more focused shows often generate more qualified leads.

Getting value from a trade show is equally about the activities and communications before and after the show as it is about your presence at the show itself.

Here are tips for maximizing your trade show investment:

1.   Lay the Groundwork.

Set goals for each show. If you expect to meet a lot of new, potential customers, set an objective for how many new contacts you hope to make and the amount of new business you expect as a result of those leads.

Let prospects know that you will be attending an upcoming show. Send personalized emails and include all pertinent information, such as your booth number, the availability of one-on-one meetings, and the details of any presentations you are making.

Some shows will provide you with an attendee list; if so, vet the list based on your target and develop an email campaign for this segment.

2.   Look Your Best.

Trade shows are a significant investment, so make sure that your trade show booth effectively portrays your company and value proposition.

At busy trade shows, you only have a few seconds to make an impression. You may find yourself competing for attendees' attention next to an exhibit that features everything from bright lighting and projected signs to specialized, large-scale displays. So how do you stand out in the crowd?

Clear messaging and appropriate displays are critical.

a)   *Create a strong booth presence that demonstrates your value.*

Ensure that attendees can understand your products or services from several feet away. This can be achieved through strong imagery supported by a professionally-developed booth display.

b) *Arrange your booth in an attendee-friendly way.*

Ensure that your booth is approachable and has materials that support your messaging that can be seen (but not read) from a distance. For example, if you have a large booth, such as a 20' x 20' or 20' x 40', allowing some room for an attendee to walk into your booth to look at displays. If booth staff members see that an attendee is taking some time to read through materials and look at images and displays, then they can approach them and engage in conversation.

c) *Manage exhibitor materials.*

Most shows offer an exhibitor list/description/visual guide to attendees. Each show offers different exhibitor list tools—understand which tools are being made available by each show and use them to your advantage. These tools are key resources for attendees to plan which exhibitors they want to visit. Some larger shows have virtual tours in which companies can upload a logo, company description, and/or any key offers (i.e. speaker presentation, seminars, discounts for purchases/agreements). Know what your competition will be doing and plan accordingly.

This is also important for lead qualification—the quicker an attendee can understand who you are and what you do, the quicker they will decide if you are relevant to them. If attendees are able to self-qualify, you don't have to deal with irrelevant booth traffic.

3. **Have Good Staffing**

My standard staffing suggestion is one person per fifty square feet of booth space. This ensures that there is always someone ready to help attendees without making the booth look overcrowded and desperate.

Depending on the show, the number of attendees, and your booth size, having a mix of staff from the technical, business development, and senior management teams is important. It enables you to have a variety of staff to connect with attendees who are in similar functions.

4. **Do Post-Show Follow Up.**

Once the trade show has ended and your booth is packed up, the real work begins. Input new contacts into your CRM or contact database, and personally follow-up with the most serious prospects as quickly as you can; do this within 96 hours.

Depending on the contacts collected, begin the lead nurturing process. Follow up and initiate a meeting to discuss their project, send them an invitation to an upcoming webinar, or send them a case study that will interest them—whatever you need to nurture the relationship.

It's vital to make this connection as soon as possible so that the discussion you had at the trade show is still fresh in your prospects' minds.

5. **Learn and Improve**

Every trade show is different so take notes on learnings (i.e.: booth location, additional information to develop for attendees, etc.)

Take time to walk the show floor—this can be valuable for identifying best practices by other companies and reviewing other locations that may better serve you for future shows.

As trade shows decrease in B2B marketing budgets, it's even more critical for companies to maximize their presence at the shows they do attend. Define the resources you have available as an exhibitor, and always debrief with booth staff following a show to identify what the team has learned and what you will incorporate next year.

METRICS

- ☑ # of trade shows attended
- ☑ # of leads
- ☑ # of new contacts

Chapter 42—Speaking Engagements

Speaking engagements are an excellent way to establish yourself and your company as a thought leader.

There are two kinds of speaking engagements—those done at your own events (essentially a Lunch and Learn) and those at third party events (e.g. industry seminars and annual conferences). Hosting your own events is a good way to build your profile, share your knowledge, and most importantly, to gain confidence in public speaking. It's important to have a track record of speaking to large audiences in order to secure opportunities to speak at high profile events, because the organizers will ask for your speaker's bio before accepting you. They need to know that you have the experience and confidence to deliver effectively. Read Chapter 40—Executive Seminars / Lunch and Learns for additional tips.

Speaking at third party events, particularly the annual gatherings of your major industry associations, is the height of thought leadership. However, they aren't easy to secure—you typically need to build up your profile at smaller events over the course of one or two years before securing a speaking opportunity at a national or international conference. There are many smaller conferences, events, and local industry associations that are interested in booking experts who have knowledge to share. Look on LinkedIn.com and Meetup.com as well as relevant industry and trade associations for the dates of upcoming events.

Delivering a presentation at a trade show will put you in front of the right audience of industry influencers and decision makers. After your speech, attendees will often come up and speak with you directly. Your speech can serve as a subtle sales pitch—after which, prospects will seek *you* out.

Speaking at third party events provides exposure for your brand by having your name included in the conference's promotional material. Having your brand associated with the other credible names on the conference program reinforces a leadership image for your company.

A successful speaking engagement requires that you have content that is relevant, fact based, informative, and focused on the needs of your targets. For a speech topic, focus on one or two key aspects of knowledge in your company's field of expertise. Your presentation can re-purpose content from other initiatives (e.g, white papers, case studies, and blog posts). Your goal in a speaking engagement should be for your audience to get one to two key takeaways that they can implement right away or that gives them serious food for thought on an issue they're tackling.

One way to capture leads from a speaking engagement is to offer a soft copy of the materials or some other compelling follow up to those who provide their business card at the end of the presentation.

METRICS
- ☑ # of engagements per year
- ☑ # of networking/connections as a result of engagements
- ☑ # of leads (contact info gained)
- ☑ # of deals from relationships attributed to speaking engagements

Chapter 43—Telemarketing

Telemarketing (also called telephone business development, cold calling, and inside sales by some companies) has been a common B2B tactic for many years. Some consider it to be part of the sales portfolio, but I consider it marketing because it generates leads and awareness.

The purpose of telemarketing is to open the door to new prospects. For some companies, telemarketing delivers strong ROI. For many though, it isn't the best way to spend the marketing budget. The difference depends on the nature of your offer, your target market, the effort put into developing the list, and the way the calls are performed. If you offer a new technology or service that doesn't already exist in the market, telemarketing can be an effective way to educate the market about your company or solution—after all, buyers aren't going to search for you online if they don't know you have a possible solution to their pains.

Here are four questions to help identify if telemarketing might work well for your business:

1. *Can you identify your targets?*

   - Do you know which companies have a need for your product or service? Do you know which individuals or group of individuals would be the buyer?

2. *Can you get through to the target buyer?*

   - Will they answer their own phones? If they have gate-keepers or never answer their phones, it will be difficult to deliver your message to them.

3. *Do you have a clear message?*

  - Are you able to articulate your solution and the results it delivers in a few sentences that will spark interest?

4. *Is the ROI of telemarketing better than the ROI of other tactics?*

  - Does your deal size and profitability justify the cost of telemarketing? For example, if you spend $500 for every booked meeting and you get one deal for every 10 meetings, your deals would need to provide more than $5,000 in profit to break even. For some B2B companies this is easy, for others it's a huge stretch.

If you determine that telemarketing makes sense for your business, here are some tips to make it work:

Identify your targets.

- Clarify the kinds of companies you are targeting. What industry are they in (by NAICS or SIC code), what size, what geography?

- Identify the decision makers or gatekeepers for your product or service. Is it the president, the head of operations, or the office manager? Or someone else? On many calls, you'll need to ask for this person by name, title, or description so know in advance who you want to speak with.

Develop your target list. You will need several types of information to make your telemarketing efforts worthwhile. Key among them:

- Company Name
- Company URL
- Individual's Name

- Phone Number
- Email Address (optional but helpful—but be wary of regulations regarding email communications, they are changing and tightening)

Some telemarketing companies possess a target list already and can work from this. If you hire an outside business development service, they will usually build the list for you based on the parameters you provide. If you hire an independent business development contractor or in-house staff, you'll have to build the list yourself. There are many list services that will sell you company contact information. Consider InfoUSA / Canada, Dun & Bradstreet, and Scott's Directory. There are also many "shillers" of lists. The legislation for list selling have changed recently, so many companies went on an eleventh hour binge to generate revenues. These latter companies have, in my experience, a very poor understanding of list criteria and poor data. They're not worth bothering with.

Alternately, consider building your list by doing research and using services like Jigsaw.com and LinkedIn. Building your list takes longer than a simple list purchase, but it can generate much better success on the phone than a purchased list.

Establish your message. What are the key points you want to convey on your calls? What are the elements of your value proposition that you need to communicate.

Establish your screening criteria. Setting up meetings with prospects is the ideal outcome of telemarketing. However, be careful what you wish for—I have seen companies set up many meetings only to find that the meetings are with companies that are not a good fit for their product or service. While you seek to open the door through telemarketing, it's also important to ask a few questions to make sure that the meetings you book will be worthwhile.

Develop a set of scripts and follow-up collateral. Telemarketing requires a series of calls and follow-ups to be effective. How many times have you received a message from someone you don't know and not returned their call? But if they are polite and call you back a couple of times over several weeks and have a compelling offer for you, you're more likely to call them back. It's the same with telemarketing. So plan the calls, voicemails, and email follow ups. Prepare collateral to send your targets after voicemails and live conversations. Appropriate collateral might include an overview of your services, case studies, and an article on your company from a recent trade publication.

Use a CRM system to track your calls and their results. A typical telemarketing campaign will involve 200-500 calls per week. This volume of activity can't be effectively tracked on a spreadsheet. Use a CRM system to organize the campaign and make sure you can evaluate both activity and results.

Test and refine. Most campaigns require some adjustment in the first few weeks to revise the script and hone in on the message and targets that are most effective in setting up quality meetings.

Give it some time but not too much. Telemarketing will work well for some companies and not for others. If it's going to work well for your business, you'll know within two months. The first couple of weeks are usually a process of refining the message and targets, and the second two weeks begin to generate some interest. Then you should start to see meetings being booked. If not, there may be an issue with your list or telemarketer. If you are confident that your list includes the right targets, then you'll have to consider whether you have the right resource doing the work or if telemarketing is simply not where you should focus your marketing effort.

METRICS
- ☑ # of calls
- ☑ # of meetings
- ☑ # of new clients
- ☑ Deal size

Chapter 44—Customer Appreciation Events

In some industries, it's all about the party. Events, like customer appreciation events, can be a good (expected even) way to build relationships with customers. In other industries, they fall flat.

Extravagant parties have been on the decline in recent years. Between the recession and hectic lifestyles, it takes a lot to attract prospects to an event. Creativity is essential—people are busy, so they only accept the most interesting invitations.

I know of one CEO who designs his customer appreciation events to be kid-friendly. His reasoning—if customers can bring their kids, they don't have to spend time away from the family or hire a babysitter, which makes them far more likely to attend. Another CEO rents a race track and a few F3000 cars for a day (with professional drivers) and takes his top twenty customers for a day of driver training and racing. The event is not cheap to host, but he is thrilled with the ROI.

The most important thing is to do something that you're passionate about. If it's a wine tasting, you better be an oenophile. If it's a day at the race track, you should like fast cars.

When preparing the invitation list for a customer appreciation event, include current customers, customer-facing employees (internal sales support or upper management make a great impression) and some prospective customers—inviting them to a gathering of happy, satisfied customers is often the final push they need to close the deal.

The best time of day to hold customer appreciation events is in the afternoon—this accommodates people with post-work family commitments but also ensures that a successful event can run into the evening. Thursdays and Fridays are popular days to hold events, because the end of the work week is when people are most ready to relax and do something different.

At the beginning of the event, allocate some time for introductions: talk about what's new at your company in terms of products/services, personnel, and business goals. But keep it light hearted and don't sell—remember, your customers are there to have fun, and the event is to thank them.

Companies can create significant brand equity by holding a major customer appreciation event every year. If you plan an event to remember, they'll look forward to the following year, which will pay dividends in customer retention rates.

METRICS
- ☑ # of people accepting invitation
- ☑ # of guests in attendance
- ☑ Qualitative feedback from the event
- ☑ Growth in # of attendees from year to year
- ☑ Retention rates among attendees

Chapter 45—Direct Mail

Capturing the attention of today's busy business decision makers and influencers is harder than ever. There is one time of day that B2B prospects unplug from their screens and stop for a moment: when they sort their mail.

Many B2B marketers have abandoned direct mail in favour of online alternatives; they assume that because everyone is online, it means no one can be reached offline.

However, direct mail can be effective. The higher cost can be outweighed by the benefits if you have a good list and a good offer. With a bulky mail (a direct mail that is more than just an envelope, i.e. includes something that makes the package "bulky"), you're more likely to get through to new prospects, since they won't throw a package straight into the trash (which is what happens with most email from unknown senders). However, direct mail is not a silver bullet—there are a few necessary steps to make it work:

Define your objective. Are you trying to generate leads? Nurture leads? Cross sell to existing customers? Pick one objective per mailing.

Know your audience. Who is going on your target list? Your objectives will guide this. Ensure your mailers are addressed properly and are personalized.

Do the math. Plan your campaign based on the numbers—how much income and sales must the campaign generate to provide a return? Remember, the leads and sales rates matter more than the overall number of responses; many campaigns make money even with a low percentage response rate.

Build your mailing list. You can buy one or build one. I find the latter more effective for small and mid-size B2B companies, because they can focus on a small group, knowing that they have the right information for the people they're targeting. They are also able to follow up consistently with the smaller list.

Have a compelling offer. Why should prospects consider your company? A relevant answer to their unspoken "what's in it for me?" is a basic starting point.

Make it easy for them to respond. Give them calls to action that are simple. The old idea that more choices = a lower response rate is bunk; the more options you give them for responding, the higher the response rate (within reason—don't include a dozen options).

Slow and steady. Most companies send out several hundred mailings and expect the phone to ring. It doesn't. It's better to send out twenty to fifty mailings per week and have your sales team follow up with each recipient by phone within a week of the package delivery. Direct mail needs to be integrated into larger overall campaigns to deliver strong ROI.

METRICS
   ☑ # of mailings sent
   ☑ # of leads
   ☑ # of deals

Chapter 46—Print Advertisements

Social media and web 2.0 have officially been embraced by B2B companies. That said, there is still a place for traditional media.

As with everything in B2B marketing, the key is strategic thinking and quality content. Well-constructed, thoughtful pieces will still be effective, and in many industries, traditional media still plays an important role in the overall marketing plan.

With magazines and newspapers in decline, many companies have stopped or greatly reduced their print ad spending. In many cases, this makes sense—companies often used print advertising when they didn't know how else to market themselves.

But if they didn't have a goal for advertising and didn't have a well-crafted plan for achieving that goal, they very rarely accomplished anything. Print advertising works as long as ads are well designed with a specific purpose in mind. An important rule in advertising is "frequency over reach". It's better to run four quarter page ads in a publication that is focused on your target market than it is to place a single full page ad in a national newspaper. In fact, if you only have enough budget to run an ad once, I would say don't bother—put that spend elsewhere. People need to see something five to seven times before it registers. This means that if you can't get on the radar of your target market five to seven times in a three to six month period, your message is falling on deaf ears.

Here are some tips on using print to deliver ROI:

1. **Be bold**. If you're going to use print, go bold to stand out. Print ads are too easy to ignore otherwise.

2. **Use simple layouts**. The most effective ads are the simplest. Headlines are short yet powerful, and the image tells a quick story. A layout that is too busy or complicated will be ignored.

3. **Keep the copy simple**. Complicated copy lowers readership. Replace large blocks of print with short paragraphs and bullet points. Don't place text over images or use light text on a dark background. Use a serif font, such as Times New Roman or Georgia, to increase readability as long as it's consistent with your brand.

4. **Focus on "you", not "we"**. "We" statements make for poor ad copy. Writing "you" statements keeps ad and copy focused on the target markets' needs.

5. **Have a good flow**. We read from top to bottom and left to right—an ad that ignores this basic "flow" looks confusing and is difficult to understand.

6. **Include a call to action**. Give people something to do: "download our free report", "call today to arrange a sales consultation", "request a free sample", etc.

METRICS

☑ # of leads—track this by including a designated phone number or URL in the ad, so you'll know where the traffic originated

☑ Ad mentions—customers will often say they saw your ad in XYZ publication

Chapter 47—Awards

Awards can be very effective B2B marketing tools, because they provide third party credibility: someone else thinks you've done well. They also give you a chance to toot your own horn to prospects and customers—or at least communicate that someone else is tooting it for you.

There are all kinds of awards for B2B companies. Some are within a single industry, and others are across multiple industries. There are awards to recognize innovation, exporting, HR, sustainability, growth, and many other accomplishments.

Like any marketing tactic, obtaining awards takes resources, namely time: time to research opportunities, time to complete the applications, and time to promote the wins. Remember that application processes (and potentially fees) will vary, so be sure to read the fine print.

Here are a few tips to help you make the most of awards:

1. Research award opportunities. Develop a list of potential award opportunities; begin with reputable industry associations, popular trade publications, and conferences as they often have awards programs. Look for awards that align with your strategic initiatives or value proposition (for example, if you're an architectural firm, look for awards that honour and showcase excellence in design, or if your firm prides itself on its ability to design and develop innovative products, identify awards within your industry that honour and feature innovation).

2. Focus on just a few awards. Awards applications are time consuming so focus on ones your firm has a good shot at. Industry awards are usually good opportunities, because they are vertical specific, and you'll have greater insight into the criteria for the award and the strength of the competition. If your industry has volumes of awards to choose from, select the ones that are the most credible and would be seen as significant by your customer and prospect base.

3. Schedule the time required for the application process and fees. Like any marketing tactic, award applications should be part of the marketing timetable. Add application due dates and other details (like who is going to complete the application, questions that may require approval from various stakeholders, and specific technical details that need to be included) to your calendar, and make sure to hit deadlines.

4. Promote your wins! From a B2B marketing perspective, it isn't winning the award that's important but promoting your win.

Here are a few ways to do that:

- Add it to your website
- Do a press release
- Include an announcement in your upcoming newsletter
- Add it as a postscript on your email signature
- Add the logo to your business card/trade show booth/website
- Hold a special event to celebrate and thank customers
- Display the award or certificate in your boardroom or other client meeting area
- Include it in the "About" section of press releases, white papers, and articles

Set a goal for the one major award you want to achieve. It may not be feasible now, but use it as something to strive for—it can be very motivating and can spur organizational development.

Awards reinforce other marketing efforts. They give sales additional support when making their next call or walking a prospect through your product/service offering.

METRICS
    ☑   # of awards applied / # of awards won

Chapter 48—Mass Media Tactics
(Radio, TV, Out of Home)

These tactics may seem like familiar marketing, because they are so prevalent in the B2C world. But in B2B they are much less common, because they reach a broad audience and therefore come at a significant cost—and for most B2Bs the ROI isn't sufficient.

Radio

Radio can be a great tactic for B2B if there is a local target market, and there is a station that aligns with what you offer—the business or news stations on the AM may be effective. That said, I don't usually see radio included in the plans of B2B companies who have a marketing budget under one million.

TV

TV is also not commonly used for B2B. TV has been the mainstay of B2C, because it enabled companies to reach large audiences. But commercials are expensive to produce and even more expensive to air. Because B2B companies target buyers in niches, it's rare that TV makes sense for a B2B company. The results of TV can be very strong but only if you have the mega budget to undertake it.

Out Of Home

"Out Of Home" marketing (billboards, for example) is usually prohibitively expensive for small and midsize B2B companies, and it delivers poor ROI. The cost associated with creating and designing ads, and then placing them, limits this tactic to those with fairly broad but local target markets and the budget to support the tactic.

Chapter 49—Other Tactics

There are literally dozens of other useful, interesting, and emerging tactics in the B2B marketing arena. Every quarter there are new ways to get the message out, get in front of customers, and demonstrate expertise. It's impossible to cover everything in this book, but I've aimed to cover the tactics you most need to know.

If there's a tactic that you've had tremendous success (or failure) with, and you think it absolutely must be covered, let me know—lisa@marketsmartb2b.com. I promise to try to include it in a future blog or article.

CONCLUSION

Getting smart about B2B marketing and reaping the rewards

If there is one thing I hope you take away from this book, it is this: <u>smart marketing, used effectively in B2B companies, leads to growth.</u>

Too many B2B companies overlook marketing, because they haven't known how to do it well. Marketing can transform a small player into an industry leader, and make the difference between struggling for sales and having leads come to you.

Small and midsize B2B companies face unique challenges when it comes to marketing. Their executive teams simply don't have the time or resources, and they rarely have the expertise to build a realistic and useful strategy and action plan—let alone execute it. And most marketing education, training, and writing is oriented to B2C industries so relatively few people have B2B experience and expertise.

There are different approaches to making marketing work for your business. Investigate the options, talk to potential service providers, and find a solution that works for you. There are ways to start at a modest level and grow the marketing along with your success. Choose an approach and develop a strategy that you're comfortable with. Give it time to achieve results (six to twelve months). You can recalibrate from there.

I would love to hear your questions and success stories. Send them to me at:

- Email: lisa@marketsmartb2b.com
- Twitter: @MezzLisa

Made in the USA
Lexington, KY
31 January 2013